REGINA CAELI

Pope Benedict XVI

REGINA CAELI

REFLECTIONS ON OUR LADY

Extracts from his writings and speeches selected by Fr Gerard Skinner

FAMILY PUBLICATIONS

ISBN 978 1 907380 05 1

This book was supported by a generous donation from the Charlotte Marshall Charitable Trust

published by
Family Publications
Denis Riches House, 66 Sandford Lane,
Kennington, Oxford OX1 5RP
www.familypublications.co.uk

Printed in England
by Cromwell Press Group, Trowbridge

Contents

Introduction

"Exalted by the Lord as Queen over all things, that she might be the more fully conformed to her Son, the Lord of lords (cf. Rv 19: 16) and conqueror of sin and death" (*Lumen Gentium*, n. 59), the Immaculate Virgin, Queen of Heaven, enjoys already the fullness of life that one day we too hope to share.

Reading Pope Benedict XVI's reflections on the mysteries of God in the life of the Blessed Virgin Mary one cannot help but be struck by the Pope's joy and love in contemplating her, particularly celebrating the glorious solemnity of the Assumption, that summer celebration of the Paschal victory of Christ.

In the following pages Pope Benedict invites us to imitate the Blessed Virgin's totally obedient response to the Lord so that we may also share in her joy in the eternal life and light of heaven.

Fr Gerard Skinner
London
Feast of the Chair of St Peter, 2010

I

IMMACULATE CONCEPTION

Homily given at the

CAPPELLA PAPALE ON THE FORTIETH ANNIVERSARY OF THE CLOSURE OF THE SECOND VATICAN COUNCIL

Solemnity of the
Immaculate Conception of the Blessed Virgin Mary
Thursday, 8 December 2005

Pope Paul VI solemnly concluded the Second Vatican Council in the square in front of St Peter's Basilica 40 years ago, on 8 December 1965. It had been inaugurated, in accordance with John XXIII's wishes, on 11 October 1962, which was then the Feast of Mary's Motherhood, and ended on the day of the Immaculate Conception.

The Council took place in a Marian setting. It was actually far more than a setting: it was the orientation of its entire process.

It refers us, as it referred the Council Fathers at that time, to the image of the Virgin who listens and lives in the Word of God, who cherishes in her heart the words that God addresses to her and, piecing them together like a mosaic, learns to understand them (cf. Lk 2: 19, 51).

It refers us to the great Believer who, full of faith, put herself in God's hands, abandoning herself to his will; it refers us to the humble Mother who, when the Son's mission so required, became part of it, and at the same time, to the courageous woman who stood beneath the Cross while the disciples fled.

In his Discourse on the occasion of the promulgation of the Dogmatic Constitution on the Church, Paul VI described Mary as *"tutrix huius Concilii"* – "Patroness of this Council" (cf. *Oecumenicum Concilium Vaticanum II, Constitutiones Decreta Declarationes,* Vatican City, 1966, p. 983) and, with an unmistakable allusion to the account of Pentecost transmitted by Luke (cf. Acts 1: 12-14), said that the Fathers were gathered in the Council Hall "*cum Maria, Matre Iesu*"* and would also have left it in her name (p. 985).

Indelibly printed in my memory is the moment when, hearing his words: "*Mariam Sanctissimam declaramus Matrem Ecclesiae*" – "We declare Mary the Most Holy Mother of the Church", the Fathers spontaneously rose at once and paid homage to the Mother of God, to our Mother, to the Mother of the Church, with a standing ovation.

Indeed, with this title the Pope summed up the Marian teaching of the Council and provided the key to understanding it. Not only does Mary have a unique relationship with Christ, the Son of God who, as man, chose to become her Son. Since she was totally united to Christ, she also totally belongs to us. Yes, we can say that Mary is close to us as no other human being is, because Christ becomes man for all men and women and his entire being is "being here for us".

Christ, the Fathers said, as the Head, is inseparable from his Body which is the Church, forming with her, so to speak, a single living subject. The Mother of the Head is also the Mother of all the Church; she is, so to speak, totally emptied of herself; she has given herself entirely to Christ and with him is given as a gift to us all. Indeed, the more the human person gives himself, the more he finds himself.

The Council intended to tell us this: Mary is so interwoven

---

* "with Mary, the Mother of Jesus."

in the great mystery of the Church that she and the Church are inseparable, just as she and Christ are inseparable. Mary mirrors the Church, anticipates the Church in her person, and in all the turbulence that affects the suffering, struggling Church she always remains the Star of salvation. In her lies the true centre in which we trust, even if its peripheries very often weigh on our soul.

In the context of the promulgation of the Constitution on the Church, Paul VI shed light on all this through a new title deeply rooted in Tradition, precisely with the intention of illuminating the inner structure of the Church's teaching, which was developed at the Council. The Second Vatican Council had to pronounce on the institutional components of the Church: on the Bishops and on the Pontiff, on the priests, lay people and Religious, in their communion and in their relations; it had to describe the Church journeying on, "clasping sinners to her bosom, at once holy and always in need of purification . . ." (*Lumen Gentium*, n. 8).

This 'Petrine' aspect of the Church, however, is included in that 'Marian' aspect. In Mary, the Immaculate, we find the essence of the Church without distortion. We ourselves must learn from her to become 'ecclesial souls', as the Fathers said, so that we too may be able, in accordance with St Paul's words, to present ourselves 'blameless' in the sight of the Lord, as he wanted us from the very beginning (cf. Col 1: 21; Eph 1: 4).

But now we must ask ourselves: What does 'Mary, the Immaculate' mean? Does this title have something to tell us? Today, the liturgy illuminates the content of these words for us in two great images.

First of all comes the marvellous narrative of the annunciation of the Messiah's coming to Mary, the Virgin of Nazareth. The Angel's greeting is interwoven with threads from the Old Testament, especially from the Prophet Zephaniah. He shows that Mary, the humble provincial woman who comes from a priestly race and bears within her the great priestly patrimony of Israel, is "the holy remnant" of Israel to which the prophets referred in all the periods of trial and darkness.

In her is present the true Zion, the pure, living dwelling-place of God. In her the Lord dwells, in her he finds the place of his repose. She is the living house of God, who does not dwell in buildings of stone but in the heart of living man. She is the shoot which sprouts from the stump of David in the dark winter night of history. In her, the words of the Psalm are fulfilled: "*The earth has yielded its fruits*" (Ps 67: 7).

She is the offshoot from which grew the tree of redemption and of the redeemed. God has not failed, as it might have seemed formerly at the beginning of history with Adam and Eve or during the period of the Babylonian Exile, and as it seemed anew in Mary's time when Israel had become a people with no importance in an occupied region and with very few recognizable signs of its holiness.

God did not fail. In the humility of the house in Nazareth lived holy Israel, the pure remnant. God saved and saves his people. From the felled tree trunk Israel's history shone out anew, becoming a living force that guides and pervades the world.

Mary is holy Israel: she says 'yes' to the Lord, she puts herself totally at his disposal and thus becomes the living temple of God.

The second image is much more difficult and obscure. This metaphor from the Book of Genesis speaks to us from a great historical distance and can only be explained with difficulty; only in the course of history has it been possible to develop a deeper understanding of what it refers to.

It was foretold that the struggle between humanity and the serpent, that is, between man and the forces of evil and death, would continue throughout history.

It was also foretold, however, that the "offspring" of a woman would one day triumph and would crush the head of the serpent to death; it was foretold that the offspring of the woman – and in this offspring the woman and the mother herself – would be victorious and that thus, through man, God would triumph.

If we set ourselves with the believing and praying Church to listen to this text, then we can begin to understand what original sin, inherited sin, is and also what the protection against this inherited sin is, what redemption is.

What picture does this passage show us? The human being does not trust God. Tempted by the serpent, he harbours the suspicion that, in the end, God takes something away from his life, that God is a rival who curtails our freedom and that we will be fully human only when we have cast him aside; in brief, that only in this way can we fully achieve our freedom.

The human being lives in the suspicion that God's love creates a dependence and that he must rid himself of this dependency if he is to be fully himself. Man does not want to receive his existence and the fullness of his life from God.

He himself wants to obtain from the tree of knowledge the power to shape the world, to make himself a god, raising himself to God's level, and to overcome death and darkness with his own efforts. He does not want to rely on love that to him seems untrustworthy; he relies solely on his own knowledge since it confers power upon him. Rather than on love, he sets his sights on power, with which he desires to take his own life autonomously in hand. And in doing so, he trusts in deceit rather than in truth and thereby sinks with his life into emptiness, into death.

Love is not dependence but a gift that makes us live. The freedom of a human being is the freedom of a limited being, and therefore is itself limited. We can possess it only as a shared freedom, in the communion of freedom: only if we live in the right way, with one another and for one another, can freedom develop.

We live in the right way if we live in accordance with the truth of our being, and that is, in accordance with God's will. For God's will is not a law for the human being imposed from the outside and that constrains him, but the intrinsic measure of his nature, a measure that is engraved within him and makes him the image of God, hence, a free creature.

If we live in opposition to love and against the truth – in opposition to God – then we destroy one another and destroy the world. Then we do not find life but act in the interests of death. All this is recounted with immortal images in the history of the original fall of man and the expulsion of man from the earthly Paradise.

Dear brothers and sisters, if we sincerely reflect about ourselves and our history, we have to say that with this narrative is described not only the history of the beginning but the history of all times, and that we all carry within us a drop of the poison of that way of thinking, illustrated by the images in the Book of Genesis.

We call this drop of poison 'original sin'. Precisely on the Feast of the Immaculate Conception, we have a lurking suspicion that a person who does not sin must really be basically boring and that something is missing from his life: the dramatic dimension of being autonomous; that the freedom to say no, to descend into the shadows of sin and to want to do things on one's own is part of being truly human; that only then can we make the most of all the vastness and depth of our being men and women, of being truly ourselves; that we should put this freedom to the test, even in opposition to God, in order to become, in reality, fully ourselves.

In a word, we think that evil is basically good, we think that we need it, at least a little, in order to experience the fullness of being. We think that Mephistopheles – the tempter – is right when he says he is the power "that always wants evil and always does good" (J.W. von Goethe, *Faust* I, 3). We think that a little bargaining with evil, keeping for oneself a little freedom against God, is basically a good thing, perhaps even necessary.

If we look, however, at the world that surrounds us we can see that this is not so; in other words, that evil is always poisonous, does not uplift human beings but degrades and humiliates them. It does not make them any the greater, purer or wealthier, but harms and belittles them.

This is something we should indeed learn on the day of the Immaculate Conception: the person who abandons himself totally in God's hands does not become God's puppet, a boring 'yes man'; he does not lose his freedom. Only the person who entrusts himself totally to God finds true freedom, the great, creative immensity of the freedom of good.

The person who turns to God does not become smaller but greater, for through God and with God he becomes great, he becomes divine, he becomes truly himself. The person who puts himself in God's hands does not distance himself from others, withdrawing into his private salvation; on the contrary, it is only then that his heart truly awakens and he becomes a sensitive, hence, benevolent and open person.

The closer a person is to God, the closer he is to people. We see this in Mary. The fact that she is totally with God is the reason why she is so close to human beings.

For this reason she can be the Mother of every consolation and every help, a Mother whom anyone can dare to address in any kind of need in weakness and in sin, for she has understanding for everything and is for everyone the open power of creative goodness.

In her, God has impressed his own image, the image of the One who follows the lost sheep even up into the mountains and among the briars and thornbushes of the sins of this world, letting himself be spiked by the crown of thorns of these sins in order to take the sheep on his shoulders and bring it home.

As a merciful Mother, Mary is the anticipated figure and everlasting portrait of the Son. Thus, we see that the image of the Sorrowful Virgin, of the Mother who shares her suffering and her love, is also a true image of the Immaculate Conception. Her heart was enlarged by being and feeling together with God. In her, God's goodness came very close to us.

Mary thus stands before us as a sign of comfort, encouragement and hope. She turns to us, saying: "Have the courage to dare with God! Try it! Do not be afraid of him! Have the courage to risk with faith! Have the courage to risk with goodness! Have the courage to risk with a pure heart! Commit yourselves to God, then you will see that it is precisely by doing so that your life will become broad and light, not boring but filled with infinite surprises, for God's infinite goodness is never depleted!"

On this Feast Day, let us thank the Lord for the great sign of his goodness which he has given us in Mary, his Mother and the Mother of the Church. Let us pray to him to put Mary on our path like a light that also helps us to become a light and to carry this light into the nights of history. Amen.

Homage of the Holy Father
to the Immaculate in 'Piazza di Spagna'

PRAYER OF HIS HOLINESS BENEDICT XVI

Thursday, 8 December 2005

On this day dedicated to Mary I have come, for the first time as Successor of Peter, to the feet of the statue of the Immaculate here in *Piazza di Spagna,* continuing the pilgrimage made many times by my Predecessors. I feel that I am accompanied by the devotion and affection of the Church living in this city of Rome and in the entire world. I bring with me the concerns and hopes of present-day humanity and come to lay them at the feet of the heavenly Mother of the Redeemer.

On this remarkable day, the 40th anniversary of the closing of the Second Vatican Council, my thought goes to 8 December 1965 when, exactly at the end of the Homily during the Eucharistic celebration in St Peter's Square, the Servant of God Paul VI addressed his thought to Mary, "the Mother of God and our spiritual Mother . . . , the creature in whom the image of God is reflected with absolute clarity, without any disturbance as happens in every other human creature."

The Pope then asked: "Is it not perhaps in directing our gaze on this woman who is our humble sister and at the same time our heavenly Mother and Queen, the spotless and sacred mirror of infinite beauty, that we can . . . [begin] our post-conciliar work? Does not the beauty of Mary Immaculate become for us an inspiring model, a comforting hope?"

He then concluded: ". . . we think it is so for us and for you.

And this is our most exalted and, God willing, our most valuable parting wish" (cf. *The Teachings of Pope Paul VI,* III, 1965).

Recalling the many events that have marked the last 40 years, how can we not relive today the various moments that have highlighted the Church's journey in this period? Mary sustained the Pastors, and in the first place the Successors of Peter, in their demanding ministry at the service of the Gospel during these 40 years; she guided the Church towards the faithful understanding and application of the conciliar Documents.

For this reason, serving as spokesperson for the entire Ecclesial Community, I wish to thank the Most Holy Virgin and I turn to her with the same sentiments that animated the Council Fathers, who dedicated to Mary the last chapter of the Dogmatic Constitution *Lumen Gentium*, underlining the inseparable relationship that unites the Virgin to the Church.

Yes, we want to thank you, Virgin Mother of God and our most beloved Mother, for your intercession for the good of the Church. You, who in embracing the divine will without reserve were consecrated with all of your energies to the person and work of your Son, teach us to keep in our heart and to meditate in silence, as you did, upon the mysteries of Christ's life.

May you who reached Calvary, ever-deeply united to your Son who from the Cross gave you as mother to the disciple John, also make us feel you are always close in each moment of our lives, especially in times of darkness and trial.

You, who at Pentecost, together with the Apostles in prayer, called upon the gift of the Holy Spirit for the newborn Church, help us to persevere in the faithful following of Christ. To you, a "sign of certain hope and comfort", we trustfully turn our gaze "until the day of the Lord shall come" (*Lumen Gentium*, n. 68).

You, Mary, are invoked with the insistent prayer of the faithful throughout the world so that you, exalted above all the angels and saints, will intercede before your Son for us, "until all families of peoples, whether they are honoured with the title of Christian or whether they still do not know the Saviour, may be happily gathered together in peace and harmony into one People of God, for the glory of the Most Holy and Undivided Trinity" (ibid., n. 69). Amen.

Tribute of the Holy Father
to Mary Immaculate

PRAYER OF HIS HOLINESS BENEDICT XVI

Spanish Steps, Rome
Friday, 8 December 2006

O Mary, Immaculate Virgin,

Again this year, with filial love, we meet at the foot of your image to renew to you the homage of the Christian community and of the city of Rome. Let us pause in prayer here, following the tradition inaugurated by previous Popes, on the solemn day in which the liturgy celebrates your Immaculate Conception, a mystery that is a source of joy and hope for all the redeemed.

We greet you and call upon you with the Angel's words: "full of grace" (Lk 1: 28), the most beautiful name that God himself has called you from eternity.

Full of grace are you, Mary, full of divine love from the very first moment of your existence, providentially predestined to be Mother of the Redeemer and intimately connected to him in the mystery of salvation.

In your Immaculate Conception shines forth the vocation of Christ's disciples, called to become, with his grace, saints and immaculate through love (cf. Eph 1: 4). In you shines the dignity of every human being who is always precious in the Creator's eyes.

Those who look to you, All Holy Mother, never lose their serenity, no matter what the hardships of life.

Although the experience of sin is a sad one since it disfigures the dignity of God's children, anyone who turns to you discovers the beauty of truth and love and finds the path that leads to the Father's house.

Full of grace, are you, Mary, which, welcoming with your 'yes' to the Creator's plan, opened to us the path of salvation. Teach us also at your school to say our 'yes' to the Lord's will. Let it be a 'yes' that joins with your own 'yes', without reservations or shadows, a 'yes' that the Heavenly Father willed to have need of in order to beget the new Man, Christ, the one Saviour of the world and of history.

Give us the courage to say 'no' to the deceptions of power, money, pleasure; to dishonest earnings, corruption and hypocrisy, to selfishness and violence; 'no' to the Evil One, the deceitful prince of this world; to say 'yes' to Christ, who destroys the power of evil with the omnipotence of love. We know that only hearts converted to Love, which is God, can build a better future for all.

Full of grace, are you, Mary! For all generations your name is a pledge of sure hope. Yes! Because as the great poet, Dante, wrote, for us mortals you are "a source of living hope" (*Paradise,* XXXIII, 12). Let us come once again as trusting pilgrims to draw faith and comfort, joy and love, safety and peace from this source, the wellspring of your Immaculate Heart.

Virgin "full of grace", show yourself to be a tender and caring Mother to those who live in this city of yours, so that the true Gospel spirit may enliven and guide their conduct; show yourself as Mother and watchful keeper of Italy and Europe, so that people may draw from their ancient Christian roots fresh vigour to build their present and their future; show yourself as a provident and merciful Mother to the whole world so that, by respecting human dignity and rejecting every form of violence and exploitation, sound foundations may be laid for the civilization of love.

Show yourself as Mother, especially to those most in need: the defenceless, the marginalized and outcasts, to the victims of a society that all too often sacrifices the human person for other ends and interests.

Show yourself, O Mary, as Mother of all, and give us Christ, the Hope of the world! "*Monstra Te esse Matrem*", O Virgin Immaculate, full of grace! Amen.

From the address given at the

ACT OF VENERATION TO THE IMMACULATE AT THE SPANISH STEPS

Solemnity of the Immaculate Conception
Saturday, 8 December 2007

At an event which has now become a tradition, we are meeting here at the Spanish Steps to offer our floral tribute to Our Lady on the day when the whole Church celebrates the feast of her Immaculate Conception. Following in the footsteps of my Predecessors, I also join you, dear faithful of Rome, to pause at Mary's feet with filial affection and love. For 150 years she has watched over our city from the top of this pillar. Today's act is a gesture of faith and devotion which our Christian community repeats from year to year, as if to reaffirm its commitment of fidelity to she who in every circumstance of daily life assures us of her help and motherly protection.

This expression of piety is at the same time an opportunity to offer to all who live in Rome or who are spending a few days as pilgrims and tourists, an opportunity, despite the diversity of cultures, to feel they are one family gathered around a Mother who has shared the daily efforts of every woman and mother of a family. She is, however, a completely singular mother, for she was chosen in advance by God for a unique and mysterious mission: to bring forth to earthly life the Father's Eternal Word, who came into the world for the salvation of all people. And Mary, Immaculate in her conception – this is how we venerate her today

– travelled her earthly pilgrimage sustained by undaunted faith, steadfast hope and humble and boundless love, following in the footsteps of her Son, Jesus. She was close to him with motherly solicitude from his birth to Calvary, where she witnessed his crucifixion, transfixed by suffering but with unwavering hope. She then experienced the joy of the Resurrection, at dawn on the third day, the new day, when the Crucified One left the tomb, overcoming for ever and definitively the power of sin and death.

Mary, in whose virginal womb God was made man, is our Mother. Indeed, from the Cross before bringing his sacrifice to completion, Jesus gave her to us as our Mother and entrusted us to her as her children. This is a mystery of mercy and love, a gift that enriches the Church with fruitful spiritual motherhood. Let us turn our gaze to her, especially today, dear brothers and sisters, and imploring her help, prepare ourselves to treasure all her maternal teaching. Does not our Heavenly Mother invite us to shun evil and to do good, following with docility the divine law engraved in every Christian's heart? Does not she, who preserved her hope even at the peak of her trial, ask us not to lose heart when suffering and death come knocking at the door of our homes? Does she not ask us to look confidently to our future? Does not the Immaculate Virgin exhort us to be brothers and sisters to one another, all united by the commitment to build together a world that is more just, supportive and peaceful?

Yes, dear friends! On this solemn day, the Church once again holds up Mary to the world as a sign of sure hope and of the definitive victory of good over evil. The one whom we invoke as "full of grace" reminds us that we are all brothers and sisters and that God is our Creator and our Father. Without him, or even worse, against him, we human beings will never be able to find the way that leads to love, we will never be able to defeat the power of hatred and violence, we will never be able to build a lasting peace.

May the people of every nation and culture welcome this message of light and hope: may they accept it as a gift from the hands of Mary, Mother of all humanity. If life is a journey and this journey is often dark, difficult and exhausting, what star can illuminate it? In my Encyclical *Spe Salvi*, published at the beginning of Advent, I wrote that the Church looks to Mary and calls on her as a "star of hope" (n. 49). During our common voyage on the sea of history, we stand in need of "lights of hope", that is, of people who shine with Christ's light and "so guide us along our way" (ibid.). And who could be a better "Star of Hope" for us than Mary? With her 'yes', with the generous offering of freedom received from the Creator, she enabled the hope of the millennia to become reality, to enter this world and its history. Through her God took flesh, became one of us and pitched his tent among us.

Thus, inspired by filial trust, we say to her: "Teach us, Mary, to believe, to hope, to love with you; show us the way that leads to peace, the way to the Kingdom of Jesus. You, Star of Hope, who wait for us anxiously in the everlasting light of the eternal Homeland, shine upon us and guide us through daily events, now and at the hour of our death. Amen!"

I join the pilgrims who have gathered at the Marian Shrines of Lourdes and Fourvière to honour the Virgin Mary in this Jubilee Year of the 150th anniversary of Our Lady's apparitions to St Bernadette. Thanks to their trust in Mary and her example, these pilgrims will become true disciples of the Saviour. With their pilgrimages they offer the many faces of the Church to those who are seeking and who come to visit the shrines. On their spiritual journey they are called to demonstrate the grace of their Baptism, to be nourished with the Eucharist, to find in prayer the strength for witness and solidarity with all their brothers and sisters in humanity. May shrines develop their vocation to prayer and to offering hospitality to people who desire to rediscover the path to God, especially through the Sacrament of Forgiveness. I also address my cordial greetings to all those, in particular young people, who are joyfully celebrating the feast of the Immaculate Conception.

Address given during the

HOMAGE TO THE IMMACULATE AT THE SPANISH STEPS

Solemnity of the Immaculate Conception
Monday, 8 December 2008

About three months ago I had the joy of going on pilgrimage to Lourdes, on the occasion of the 150th anniversary of the historical apparitions of the Virgin Mary to St Bernadette. The celebration of this unique anniversary ends precisely today on the Solemnity of the Immaculate Conception, because in showing herself to Bernadette for the last time in the Grotto of Massabielle, the "beautiful Lady", as Bernadette called her, revealed her name, saying "I am the Immaculate Conception." She said this in the local dialect and the little visionary related the phrase, to her unknown and incomprehensible, to her parish priest.

"Immaculate Conception": we too repeat that mysterious name with feeling, here, at the foot of this monument in the heart of Rome; and countless brothers and sisters of ours are doing the same in thousands of other places in the world, at shrines and in chapels as well as in Christian homes. Today, wherever a Catholic community exists, Our Lady is venerated in it with this stupendous and marvellous name: the Immaculate Conception. Of course, the conviction that Mary's conception was immaculate had already existed for centuries before the apparitions in Lourdes, which came as a heavenly seal after my venerable Predecessor, Bl. Pius IX, defined the Dogma on 8

December 1854. On today's feast, so dear to Christian people, this expression rises from hearts and is pronounced by lips as our heavenly Mother's name. Just as a child raises his eyes to his mother's face and on seeing her smile forgets every fear and every pain, so do we, turning our eyes to Mary, recognize in her 'God's smile', the immaculate reflection of divine light; in her we find new hope even in the midst of the problems and tragedies of the world.

It is a tradition that the Pope joins with the homage of the city, bringing Mary a basket of roses. These flowers express our love and devotion: the love and devotion of the Pope, of the Church of Rome and of the inhabitants of this city, who feel they are spiritual children of the Virgin Mary. Roses, symbolically, can express everything beautiful and good that we have done during the year because at this traditional encounter we all desire to offer everything to our Mother, convinced that we could not have done anything without her protection and without the graces that daily she obtains for us from God. Yet, as the saying goes, there is no rose without a thorn, and on the stems of these magnificent white roses too there is no lack of thorns that represent for us difficulty and suffering, the troubles that have marked and still mark people's lives and the life of our community. Joys are presented to our Mother but anxieties are also entrusted to her, since the faithful are confident that they will find comfort and support in her to go forward, so as not to be disheartened.

O Immaculate Virgin, at this moment I would especially like to entrust to you the 'little ones' of our city: the children, first of all, and above all those who are seriously ill, children who are disabled and those who are suffering the consequences of oppressive family situations. Watch over them and grant that they may feel the warmth of God's love in the affection and help of those who are beside them! To you, O Mary, I entrust the lonely elderly, the sick, immigrants who find it hard to adjust, families that find it difficult to make ends meet and people who cannot find employment or who have lost a job indispensable for their survival. Teach us, Mary, to show solidarity with those in difficulty, to fill the ever increasing social gaps. Help us to foster a more lively sense of the common good, of respect for that which is public, and spur us to view the city and more than ever our City of Rome as the patrimony of all, making each one of us do our part, to build a more just and supportive society with awareness and commitment.

O Immaculate Mother, who are a sign of certain hope and comfort to everyone, help us to let ourselves be attracted by your immaculate purity. Your beauty, *Tota Pulchra,*[*] as we sing today, assures us that the victory of love is possible; indeed, that it is certain. It assures us that grace is stronger than sin, and that redemption from any form of slavery is therefore possible. Yes, O Mary, help us to believe with greater trust in good, to wager on giving freely, on service, on non-violence, on the power of the truth. Encourage us to be alert, not to give into the temptation of easy evasions, to face reality and its problems with courage and responsibility. This is what you did, a young woman called to stake everything on the Word of the Lord. May you be a loving mother for our young people, so that they may have the courage to be "watchmen of the dawn", and give this virtue to all Christians so that they may be the heart of the world in this difficult period of history. Virgin Immaculate, Mother of God and our Mother, *Salus Populi Romani,*[†] pray for us!

---

* "Thou art all fair".

† "Health [Protectress] of the Roman People".

ANGELUS

Solemnity of the Immaculate Conception of the Blessed Virgin Mary

St Peter's Square, Tuesday, 8 December 2009

On 8 December we celebrate one of the most beautiful Feasts of the Blessed Virgin Mary: the Solemnity of the Immaculate Conception. But what does Mary being 'Immaculate' mean? And what does this title tell us? First of all let us refer to the biblical texts of today's Liturgy, especially the great 'fresco' of the third chapter of the book of Genesis and the account of the Annunciation in the Gospel according to Luke. After the original sin, God addresses the serpent, which represents Satan, curses it and adds a promise: "I will put enmity between you and the woman, and between your seed and her seed; he shall bruise your head, and you shall bruise his heel" (Gn 3: 15). It is the announcement of revenge: at the dawn of the Creation, Satan seems to have the upper hand, but the son of a woman is to crush his head. Thus, through the offspring of a woman, God himself will triumph. Goodness will triumph. That woman is the Virgin Mary of whom was born Jesus Christ who, with his sacrifice, defeated the ancient tempter once and for all. This is why in so many paintings and statues of the Virgin Immaculate she is portrayed in the act of crushing a serpent with her foot.

Luke the Evangelist, on the other hand, shows the Virgin Mary receiving the Annunciation of the heavenly Messenger (cf. Lk 1: 26-38). She appears as the humble, authentic daughter of Israel, the true Zion in which God wishes to take up his abode. She is the shoot from which the Messiah, the just and merciful

King, is to spring. In the simplicity of the house of Nazareth dwells the pure "remnant" of Israel from which God wants his People to be reborn, like a new tree that will spread its branches throughout the world, offering to all humanity the good fruit of salvation. Unlike Adam and Eve, Mary stays obedient to the Lord's will, with her whole being she speaks her 'yes' and makes herself entirely available to the divine plan. She is the new Eve, the true "mother of all the living", namely, those who, because of their faith in Christ, receive eternal life.

Dear friends, what an immense joy to have Mary Immaculate as our Mother! Every time we experience our frailty and the promptings of evil, we may turn to her and our hearts receive light and comfort. Even in the trials of life, in the storms that cause faith and hope to vacillate, let us recall that we are her children and that our existence is deeply rooted in the infinite grace of God. Although the Church is exposed to the negative influences of the world, she always finds in Mary the star to guide her so that she may follow the route pointed out to her by Christ. Indeed, Mary is the Mother of the Church, as Pope Paul VI and the Second Vatican Council solemnly proclaimed. Therefore, while we thank God for this marvellous sign of his goodness, let us entrust to the Virgin Immaculate each one of us, our families and communities, the entire Church and the whole world.

Address given during the

HOMAGE TO THE IMMACULATE AT THE SPANISH STEPS

Solemnity of the Immaculate Conception of the Blessed Virgin Mary

Tuesday, 8 December 2009

In the heart of Christian cities, Mary is a sweet and reassuring presence. In her discreet style, she gives everyone peace and hope, both in the happy and sad moments of life. In churches, chapels or on the walls of buildings there is a painting, mosaic or a statue as a reminder of the presence of the Mother, constantly watching over her children. Here too in Piazza di Spagna, Mary is placed high up as though on guard over Rome.

What does Mary tell the city? Of what does her presence remind us? It reminds us that "where sin increased, grace abounded all the more" (Rom 5: 20), as the Apostle Paul wrote. She is the Immaculate Mother who tells people in our day too: Do not be afraid, Jesus has defeated evil, he has uprooted it, delivering us from its rule.

How great is our need of this good news! Every day, in fact, in the newspapers, on television and on the radio bad news is broadcast, repeated, amplified, so that we become used to the most terrible things and inured to them, and in a certain way poisoned, since the negative effect is never completely eliminated but accumulates day after day. The heart hardens and thoughts grow gloomy. For this reason, the city needs Mary whose presence speaks of God, reminds us of the victory of Grace over sin and leads us to hope, even in the most difficult human situations.

In the city invisible people live or survive who every now and then hit the front page headlines or television news and are exploited to the very last, as long as the news and images are newsworthy. This is a perverse mechanism which unfortunately few are able to resist. The city first hides them and then exposes them to public scrutiny, pitilessly or with false pity. Instead, there is in every person the desire to be accepted as a person and considered a sacred reality, for every human history is a sacred history and demands the utmost respect.

The city, dear brothers and sisters, is all of us! Each one of us contributes with his life to its moral atmosphere, for better or for worse. The border between good and evil runs through every heart and none of us should feel entitled to judge others. Rather, each one must feel duty bound to improve him or herself. The mass media always tends to make us feel like 'spectators', as if evil concerned only others and certain things could never happen to us. Instead, we are all 'actors' and, for better or for worse, our behaviour has an influence on others.

We often complain of the pollution of the atmosphere that in some parts of the city is unbreathable. It is true. Everyone must do his or her part to make the city a cleaner place. Yet, there is another kind of contamination, less perceptible to the senses, but equally dangerous. It is the pollution of the spirit; it makes us smile less, makes our faces gloomier, less likely to greet each other or look each other in the eye. The city has many faces but unfortunately collective dynamics can make us lose our in-depth perception of them. We perceive everything superficially. People become bodies and these bodies lose their soul, they become things, faceless objects that can be exchanged and consumed.

Mary Immaculate helps us to rediscover and defend what lies

within people, for in her is a perfect transparency of the soul in the body. She is purity in person, in the sense that spirit, soul and body are fully consistent with one another and with God's will. Our Lady teaches us to be open to God's action and to see others as he sees them: starting with the heart. And to look at them with compassion, with love, with infinite tenderness, especially those who are lonely, despised, or exploited. "Where sin increased, grace abounded all the more."

I want to pay homage publicly to all those who in silence, not with words but with deeds, strive to practise this evangelical law of love that propels the world forward. There are so many of them even here in Rome and they rarely hit the headlines. They are men and women of all ages, who have realized that it is not worth condemning, complaining or accusing; that it is better to respond to evil by doing good. This changes things; or rather it changes people, and hence improves society.

While we are busy in our daily routine, let us listen to Mary's voice. Let us hear her silent but pressing appeal. She tells each one of us that wherever sin increases, grace may abound all the more, starting in your our own heart and in your life. And the city will be more beautiful, more Christian and more human.

Thank you, Holy Mother, for your message of hope. Thank you for your silent but eloquent presence in the heart of our city. Immaculate Virgin, *Salus Populi Romani*, pray for us!

II
ANNUNCIATION

From the Homily given during the

VISIT TO THE ROMAN PARISH OF SANTA MARIA CONSOLATRICE

Fourth Sunday of Advent, 18 December 2005

Let us now meditate briefly on the most beautiful Gospel of this Fourth Sunday of Advent, which for me is one of the loveliest passages of Sacred Scripture. And so as not to take too long, I would like to reflect on only three words from this rich Gospel.

The first word on which I would like to meditate with you is the Angel's greeting to Mary. In the Italian translation the Angel says: "Hail, Mary". But the underlying Greek word, "Kaire", means in itself "be glad" or "rejoice".

And here is the first surprising thing: the greeting among the Jews was 'Shalom', 'peace', whereas the greeting of the Greek world was 'Kaire', 'be glad'. It is surprising that the Angel, on entering Mary's house, should have greeted her with the greeting of the Greeks: "Kaire", "be glad, rejoice". And when, 40 years later, the Greeks had read this Gospel, they were able to see an important message in it: they realized that the beginning of the New Testament, to which this passage from Luke referred, was bringing openness to the world of peoples and to the universality of the People of God, which by then included not only the Jewish people but also the world in its totality, all peoples. The new universality of the Kingdom of the true son of David appears in this Greek greeting of the Angel.

However, it is appropriate to point out straightaway that the

Angel's words took up a prophetic promise that is found in the Book of the Prophet Zephaniah. We find the same greeting almost literally. Inspired by God, the Prophet Zephaniah says to Israel: "Shout for joy, O daughter Zion! . . . the Lord [is with you and] is in your midst." We know that Mary was very familiar with the Sacred Scriptures. Her *Magnificat* is a fabric woven of threads from the Old Testament. We may thus be certain that the Blessed Virgin understood straightaway that these were the words of the Prophet Zephaniah addressed to Israel, to the "daughter Zion", considered as a dwelling place of God. And now the surprising thing, which must have given Mary food for thought, is that these words, addressed to all Israel, were being specifically addressed to her, Mary. And thus, it must clearly have appeared to her that she herself was the "daughter Zion" of whom the Prophet spoke, and that the Lord, therefore, had a special intention for her, that she was called to be the true dwelling place of God, a dwelling place not built of stones but of living flesh, of a living heart, that God was really intending to take her, the Virgin, as his own true temple. What an intention! And as a result, we can understand that Mary began to think with special intensity about what this greeting meant.

However, let us now reflect in particular on the first word: "Rejoice, be glad." This is the first word that resounds in the New Testament as such, because the Angel's announcement to Zechariah of the birth of John the Baptist is the word that still rings out on the threshold between the two Testaments. It is only with this dialogue which the Angel Gabriel has with Mary that the New Testament really begins. We can therefore say that the first word of the New Testament is an invitation to joy: "rejoice, be glad!" The New Testament is truly 'Gospel', the 'Good News' that brings us joy. God is not remote from us, unknown, enigmatic or perhaps dangerous. God is close to us, so close that he makes himself a child and we can informally address this God.

It was the Greek world above all that grasped this innovation, that felt this joy deeply, for it had been unclear to the Greeks whether there was a good God, a wicked God or simply no God. Religion at that time spoke to them of so many divinities: therefore, they had felt they were surrounded by very different divinities that were opposed to one another; thus, they were afraid that if they did something for one of these divinities, another might be offended and seek revenge.

So it was that they lived in a world of fear, surrounded by dangerous demons, never knowing how to save themselves from these forces in conflict with one another. It was a world of fear, a dark world. Then they heard: "Rejoice, these demons are nothing; the true God exists and this true God is good, he loves us, he knows us, he is with us, with us even to the point that he took on flesh!"

This is the great joy that Christianity proclaims. Knowing this God is truly 'Good News', a word of redemption.

Perhaps we Catholics who have always known it are no longer surprised and no longer feel this liberating joy keenly. However, if we look at today's world where God is absent, we cannot but note that it is also dominated by fears and uncertainties: is it good to be a person or not? Is it good to be alive or not? Is it truly a good to exist? Or might everything be negative? And they really live in a dark world, they need anaesthetics to be able to live. Thus, the words: "Rejoice, because God is with you, he is with us", are words that truly open a new epoch. Dear friends, with an act of faith we must once again accept and understand in the depths of our hearts this liberating word: "Rejoice!"

We cannot keep solely for ourselves this joy that we have received; joy must always be shared. Joy must be communicated. Mary went without delay to communicate her joy to her cousin Elizabeth. And ever since her Assumption into Heaven she has showered joy upon the whole world, she has become the great Consoler: our Mother who communicates joy, trust and kindness and also invites us to spread joy. This is the real commitment of Advent: to bring joy to others. Joy is the true gift of Christmas, not expensive presents that demand time and money.

We can transmit this joy simply: with a smile, with a kind gesture, with some small help, with forgiveness. Let us give this joy and the joy given will be returned to us. Let us seek in particular to communicate the deepest joy, that of knowing God in Christ. Let us pray that this presence of God's liberating joy will shine out in our lives.

The second word on which I would like to meditate is another word of the Angel's: "Do not fear, Mary", he says. In fact, there was reason for her to fear, for it was a great burden to bear the weight of the world upon herself, to be the Mother of the universal King, to be the Mother of the Son of God: what a burden that was! It was too heavy a burden for human strength to bear. But the Angel said: "Do not fear! Yes, you are carrying God, but God is carrying you. Do not fear!"

These words, "Do not fear", must have deeply penetrated Mary's heart. We can imagine how in various situations the Virgin must have pondered on those words, she must have heard them again.

At the moment when Simeon said to her: "This child is destined to be the downfall and the rise of many in Israel, a sign that will be opposed – and you yourself will be pierced with a sword", at that very moment in which she might have succumbed to fear, Mary returned to the Angel's words and felt their echo within her: "Do not fear, God is carrying you." Then, when contradictions were unleashed against Jesus during his public life and many said, "He is crazy", she thought once again of the Angel's words in her heart: "Do not fear", and went ahead. Lastly, in the encounter on the way to Calvary and then under the Cross, when all seemed to be destroyed, she again heard the Angel's words in her heart: "Do not fear". Hence, she stood courageously beside her dying Son and, sustained by faith, moved towards the Resurrection, towards Pentecost, towards the foundation of the new family of the Church.

"Do not fear": Mary also addresses these words to us. I have already pointed out that this world of ours is a world of fear: the fear of misery and poverty, the fear of illness and suffering, the fear of solitude, the fear of death. We have in this world a widely developed insurance system; it is good that it exists. But we know that at the moment of deep suffering, at the moment of the ultimate loneliness of death, no insurance policy will be able to protect us. The only valid insurance in those moments is the one that comes to us from the Lord, who also assures us: "Do not fear, I am always with you." We can fall, but in the end we fall into God's hands, and God's hands are good hands.

The third word: at the end of the conversation, Mary answered the Angel, "I am the servant of the Lord. Let it be done to me as you say." Thus, Mary anticipated the 'Our Father's' third invocation: "Your will be done". She said 'yes' to God's great will, a will apparently too great for a human being; Mary said 'yes' to this divine will, she placed herself within this will, placed her whole life with a great 'yes' within God's will, and thus opened the world's door to God.

Adam and Eve, with their 'no' to God's will, had closed this door. "Let God's will be done": Mary invites us too to say this 'yes' which sometimes seems so difficult. We are tempted to prefer our own will, but she tells us: "Be brave, you too say: 'Your will be done', because this will is good." It might at first seem an unbearable burden, a yoke impossible to bear; but in reality, God's will is not a burden, God's will gives us wings to fly high and thus we too can dare, with Mary, to open the door of our lives to God, the doors of this world, by saying 'yes' to his will, aware that this will is the true good and leads us to true happiness. Let us pray to Mary, Comfort of the Afflicted, our Mother, the Mother of the Church, to give us the courage to say this 'yes' and also to give us this joy of being with God and to lead us to his Son, to true life. Amen!

PILGRIMAGE OF
HIS HOLINESS BENEDICT XVI
TO THE HOLY LAND 8-15 MAY 2009

From the Homily given at the

CELEBRATION OF VESPERS WITH BISHOPS, PRIESTS, MEN AND WOMEN RELIGIOUS, ECCLESIAL AND PASTORAL MOVEMENTS OF GALILEE

Upper Basilica of the Annunciation, Nazareth
Thursday, 14 May 2009

It is profoundly moving for me to be present with you today in the very place where the Word of God was made flesh and came to dwell among us. How fitting that we should gather here to sing the Evening Prayer of the Church, giving praise and thanks to God for the marvels he has done for us!

What happened here in Nazareth, far from the gaze of the world, was a singular act of God, a powerful intervention in history, through which a child was conceived who was to bring salvation to the whole world. The wonder of the Incarnation continues to challenge us to open up our understanding to the limitless possibilities of God's transforming power, of his love for us, his desire to be united with us. Here the eternally begotten Son of God became man, and so made it possible for us, his brothers and sisters, to share in his divine sonship. That downward movement of self-emptying love made possible the upward movement of exaltation in which we too are raised to share in the life of God himself (cf. Phil 2:6-11).

The Spirit who "came upon Mary" (cf. Lk 1:35) is the same Spirit who hovered over the waters at the dawn of Creation (cf. Gen 1:2). We are reminded that the Incarnation was a new creative act. When our Lord Jesus Christ was conceived in Mary's virginal womb through the power of the Holy Spirit, God united himself with our created humanity, entering into a permanent new relationship with us and ushering in a new Creation. The narrative of the Annunciation illustrates God's extraordinary courtesy (cf. Mother Julian of Norwich, *Revelations* 77-79). He does not impose himself, he does not simply pre-determine the part that Mary will play in his plan for our salvation: he first seeks her consent. In the original Creation there was clearly no question of God seeking the consent of his creatures, but in this new Creation he does so. Mary stands in the place of all humanity. She speaks for us all when she responds to the Angel's invitation. Saint Bernard describes how the whole court of heaven was waiting with eager anticipation for her word of consent that consummated the nuptial union between God and humanity. The attention of all the choirs of angels was riveted on this spot, where a dialogue took place that would launch a new and definitive chapter in world history. Mary said, "Let it be done to me according to your word." And the Word of God became flesh.

When we reflect on this joyful mystery, it gives us hope, the sure hope that God will continue to reach into our history, to act with creative power so as to achieve goals which by human reckoning seem impossible. It challenges us to open ourselves to the transforming action of the Creator Spirit who makes us new, makes us one with him, and fills us with his life. It invites us, with exquisite courtesy, to consent to his dwelling within us, to welcome the Word of God into our hearts, enabling us to respond to him in love and to reach out in love towards one another.

In the State of Israel and the Palestinian Territories, Christians form a minority of the population. Perhaps at times you feel that your voice counts for little. Many of your fellow Christians have emigrated, in the hope of finding greater security and better prospects elsewhere. Your situation calls to mind that of the young virgin Mary, who led a hidden life in Nazareth, with little by way of worldly wealth or influence. Yet to quote Mary's words in her great hymn of praise, the *Magnificat*, God has looked upon his servant in her lowliness, he has filled the hungry with good things. Draw strength from Mary's canticle, which very soon we will be singing in union with the whole Church throughout the world. Have the confidence to be faithful to Christ and to remain here in the land that he sanctified with his own presence. Like Mary, you have a part to play in God's plan for salvation, by bringing Christ forth into the world, by bearing witness to him and spreading his message of peace and unity. For this, it is essential that you should be united among yourselves, so that the Church in the Holy Land can be clearly recognized as "a sign and instrument of communion with God and of the unity of the entire human race" (*Lumen Gentium*, n. 1). Your unity in faith, hope and love is a fruit of the Holy Spirit dwelling within you, enabling you to be effective instruments of God's peace, helping to build genuine reconciliation between the different peoples who recognize Abraham as their father in faith. For, as Mary joyfully proclaimed in her *Magnificat*, God is ever "mindful of his mercy, the mercy promised to our forefathers, to Abraham and his children for ever" (Lk 1:54-55).

Dear friends in Christ, be assured that I constantly remember you in my prayer, and I ask you to do the same for me. Let us turn now towards our heavenly Father, who in this place looked upon his servant in her lowliness, and let us sing his praises in union with the Blessed Virgin Mary, with all the choirs of angels and saints, and with the whole Church in every part of the world.

III
VISITATION

From the Address of His Holiness Benedict XVI for the

CONCLUSION OF THE MARIAN MONTH OF MAY

Grotto of Our Lady of Lourdes in the Vatican Gardens
Tuesday, 31 May 2005

Dear friends, you have wound your way up to the Grotto of Lourdes reciting the holy Rosary, as if to respond to the Virgin's invitation to raise your spirit towards Heaven. Our Lady accompanies us every day in our prayers. During this special Year of the Eucharist in which we are living, Mary helps us above all to discover ever better the great Sacrament of the Eucharist.

In his last Encyclical, *Ecclesia de Eucharistia,* our beloved Pope John Paul II presented her to us as "Woman of the Eucharist" throughout her life (cf. n. 53). "Woman of the Eucharist" through and through, beginning with her inner disposition: from the Annunciation, when she offered herself for the Incarnation of the Word of God, to the Cross and to the Resurrection; "Woman of the Eucharist" in the period subsequent to Pentecost, when she received in the Sacrament that Body which she had conceived and carried in her womb.

Today, in particular, we pause to meditate on the mystery of the Visitation of the Virgin to St Elizabeth. Mary, carrying in her womb the recently conceived Jesus, went to see her elderly cousin Elizabeth, whom everyone said was sterile but who instead had reached the sixth month of a pregnancy given to her by God (cf. Lk 1: 36). Mary was a young girl but she was not afraid, for God was with her, within her.

In a certain way we can say that her journey was – we like to emphasize in this Year of the Eucharist – the first 'Eucharistic procession' in history. Mary, living Tabernacle of God made flesh, is the Ark of the Covenant in whom the Lord visited and redeemed his people. Jesus' presence filled her with the Holy Spirit.

When she entered Elizabeth's house, her greeting was overflowing with grace: John leapt in his mother's womb, as if he were aware of the coming of the One whom he would one day proclaim to Israel. The children exulted, the mothers exulted. This meeting, imbued with the joy of the Holy Spirit, is expressed in the Canticle of the *Magnificat*.

Is this not also the joy of the Church, which ceaselessly welcomes Christ in the holy Eucharist and brings him into the world with the testimony of active charity, steeped in faith and hope? Yes, welcoming Jesus and bringing him to others is the true joy of Christians!

Dear Brothers and Sisters, let us follow and imitate Mary, a deeply Eucharistic soul, and our whole life can become a *Magnificat* (cf. *Ecclesia de Eucharistia,* n. 58), praise of God. May this be the grace that we ask from the Virgin Most Holy this evening at the end of the month of May.

From the Address of His Holiness Benedict XVI

FOR THE CONCLUSION OF THE MARIAN MONTH OF MAY

Grotto of Our Lady of Lourdes in the Vatican Gardens
Wednesday, 31 May 2006

I have the joy of joining you at the end of this evocative Marian Prayer Meeting. In this way, in front of the Lourdes Grotto in the Vatican Gardens, we end the month of May in this year marked by the reception of the image of Our Lady of Fatima in St Peter's Square on the 25th anniversary of the attack on beloved John Paul II.

This year is also notable for the Apostolic Journey that the Lord granted me to make to Poland, where I was able to visit the places dear to my great Predecessor.

Concerning this Pilgrimage . . . I now recall in particular my visit to the Shrine of *Jasna Góra* in Czestochowa, where I understood even better how closely our heavenly Advocate accompanies the journey of her children, and that she does not leave unheard supplications addressed to her with humility and trust.

I would like to thank her once again, with you, for having accompanied me during my visit to the beloved land of Poland.

I would also like to express to Mary my gratitude for the support she offers me in my daily service to the Church. I know that I can count on her help in every situation; indeed, I know that she foresees with maternal intuition all her children's needs and intervenes effectively to sustain them: this has been the experience of the Christian people ever since its first steps in Jerusalem.

On today's Feast of the Visitation, as in every passage of the Gospel, we see Mary docile to the divine plan and with an attitude of provident love for the brethren. In fact, the humble maiden from Nazareth, still amazed at what the Angel Gabriel had announced to her – that is, that she would be the mother of the promised Messiah – learned that her kinswoman Elizabeth had, in her old age, also conceived a son.

She immediately set out with haste for the house of her cousin, the Evangelist notes (cf. Lk 1: 39), to offer her help at a time of special need.

How can we fail to see that the hidden protagonist in the meeting between the young Mary and the by-then elderly Elizabeth is Jesus?

Mary bears him in her womb as in a sacred tabernacle and offers him as the greatest gift to Zechariah, to Elizabeth, his wife, and also to the infant developing in her womb. "Behold", the mother of John the Baptist says, "when the voice of your greeting came to my ears, the babe in my womb leaped for joy" (Lk 1: 44).

Whoever opens his or her heart to the Mother encounters and welcomes the Son and is pervaded by his joy. True Marian devotion never obscures or diminishes faith and love for Jesus Christ Our Saviour, the one Mediator between God and humankind.

On the contrary, entrustment to Our Lady is a privileged path, tested by numerous saints, for a more faithful following of the Lord. Consequently, let us entrust ourselves to her with filial abandonment.

From the Address given at the

MARIAN VIGIL FOR THE CONCLUSION OF THE MONTH OF MAY

St Peter's Square
Feast of the Visitation of the Blessed Virgin Mary
Saturday, 31 May 2008

Today we are celebrating the Feast of the Visitation of the Blessed Virgin and the memorial of the Immaculate Heart of Mary. Therefore, everything invites us to turn our trusting glance to Mary. To her, also this evening, we addressed the ancient and ever truly pious practice of the Rosary.

The Rosary, when it is not a mechanical, traditional form of repetition, is a Biblical meditation that allows us to trace the events of the Lord's life in the company of the Blessed Virgin, pondering them, like her, in our heart. In many Christian communities during the month of May there is the beautiful custom of reciting the Holy Rosary in a more solemn way in families and in parishes. Now that the month is ending, may this good habit continue. Rather, may it continue with more commitment so that, at the school of Mary, the lamp of faith may shine ever more in the hearts and homes of Christians.

In today's Feast of the Visitation the liturgy has us listen again to Luke's Gospel passage that recounts Mary of Nazareth's journey to the home of her elderly cousin Elizabeth. Let us imagine the Virgin's state of mind after the Annunciation, when the Angel left her. Mary found herself with a great mystery enclosed within her womb; she knew something extraordinarily unique had happened; she was aware that the last chapter of salvation history in the world had begun. But everything around her remained as before and the village of Nazareth was completely unaware of what had happened to her.

Before worrying about herself, Mary instead thought about elderly Elizabeth, who she knew was well on in her pregnancy, and, moved by the mystery of love that she had just welcomed within herself, she set out "in haste" to go to offer Elizabeth her help. This is the simple and sublime greatness of Mary! When she reaches Elizabeth's house, an event takes place that no artist could ever portray with the beauty and the intensity with which it took place. The interior light of the Holy Spirit enfolds their persons. And Elizabeth, enlightened from on high, exclaims: "Blessed are you among women, and blessed is the fruit of your womb! And why is this granted me, that the mother of my Lord should come to me? For behold, when the voice of your greeting came to my ears, the babe in my womb leaped for joy. And blessed is she who believed that there would be a fulfilment of what was spoken to her from the Lord" (Lk 1: 42-45).

These words could appear to us out of proportion with respect to the real context. Elizabeth is one of the many elderly people in Israel and Mary is an unknown young woman from a remote village of Galilee. What can this be and what can they accomplish in a world where other people count and other powers hold sway? Yet, once again Mary amazes us; her heart is limpid, totally open to God's light. Her soul is without sin, it is not weighed down by pride or selfishness. Elizabeth's words enkindle in her spirit a canticle of praise, which is an authentic and profound 'theological' reading of history: a reading that we must continually learn from the one whose faith is without shadow and without wrinkle. "My soul proclaims the greatness of the Lord." Mary recognizes God's greatness. This is the first indispensable sentiment of faith. It is the sentiment that gives security to human creatures and frees from fear, even in the midst of the tempest of history.

Going beyond the surface, Mary 'sees' the work of God in history with the eyes of faith. This is why she is blessed, because she believed. By faith, in fact, she accepted the Word of the Lord and conceived the Incarnate Word. Her faith has shown her that the thrones of the powerful of this world are all temporary, while God's throne is the only rock that does not change or fall. Her *Magnificat*, at the distance of centuries and millennia, remains the truest and most profound interpretation of history, while the interpretations of so many of this world's wise have been belied by events in the course of the centuries.

Dear brothers and sisters, let us return home with the *Magnificat* in our heart. Let us bring the same sentiments of praise and thanksgiving of Mary to the Lord, her faith and her hope, her docile abandonment in the hands of Divine Providence. May we imitate her example of readiness and generosity in the service of our brethren. Indeed, only by accepting God's love and making of our existence a selfless and generous service to our neighbour, can we joyfully lift a song of praise to the Lord. May the Blessed Mother, who invites us this evening to find refuge in her Immaculate Heart, obtain this grace for us.

REGINA CAELI

Saint Peter's Square
Solemnity of Pentecost Sunday, 31 May 2009

Today the Church throughout the world is reliving the Solemnity of Pentecost, the mystery of her birth, her own 'Baptism' in the Holy Spirit (cf. Acts 1:5) which occurred in Jerusalem 50 days after Easter, precisely on the Jewish Feast of Pentecost. The Risen Jesus had told his disciples: "Stay in the city, until you are clothed with power from on high" (Lk 24:49). This actually happened in the Upper Room, while they were all gathered in prayer with Mary, the Virgin Mother.

As we read in the Acts of the Apostles, that place was suddenly filled with the rush of a mighty wind and tongues as of fire settled on each one of those present. The Apostles then went out and began to proclaim in different languages that Jesus is the Christ, the Son of God, dead and risen (cf. Acts 2:1-4). The Holy Spirit, who, with the Father and the Son, created the universe, who guided the People of Israel through history and spoke through the Prophets, who in the fullness of time cooperated in our redemption, came down at Pentecost upon the nascent Church and made her missionary, sending her out to proclaim to all peoples the victory of divine love over sin and death.

The Holy Spirit is the soul of the Church. Without him what would she be reduced to? She would certainly be an important movement in history, a complex and solid social institution, perhaps a sort of humanitarian agency. And to tell the truth she is considered such by those who do not see her from a perspective of faith. Yet, the reality is that in her true nature and also in her authentic presence in history, the Church is ceaselessly formed and guided by the Spirit of her Lord. She is a living body, whose vitality is, precisely, the fruit of the invisible divine Spirit.

Dear friends, this year the Solemnity of Pentecost occurs on the last day of the month of May on which the beautiful Marian feast of the Visitation is normally celebrated. This fact invites us to let ourselves be inspired and, as it were, instructed by the Virgin Mary, who was the protagonist of both these events. In Nazareth she received the announcement of her unique motherhood and, immediately after conceiving Jesus by the power of the Holy Spirit, she was impelled by the same Spirit of love to go and help her elderly kinswoman Elizabeth, who had reached the sixth month of a pregnancy that was also miraculous. The young Mary who is carrying Jesus in her womb and who, forgetting herself, hurries to the help of her neighbour, is a wonderful image of the Church in the perennial youthfulness of the Spirit, of the missionary Church of the incarnate Word called to bring him to the world and to witness to him especially in the service of charity. Let us therefore invoke the intercession of Mary Most Holy, so that she may obtain for the Church of our time that she be powerfully strengthened by the Holy Spirit. In particular, may the ecclesial communities that are suffering persecution in Christ's name feel the comforting presence of the Paraclete so that, participating in Christ's suffering, they may receive the Spirit of glory in abundance (cf. 1 Pt 4:13-14).

IV
MOTHER OF GOD

From the Homily given on the

SOLEMNITY OF MARY, MOTHER OF GOD AND 39TH WORLD DAY OF PEACE

Vatican Basilica
Sunday, 1 January 2006

In today's liturgy our gaze continues to be turned to the great mystery of the Incarnation of the Son of God, while with particular emphasis we contemplate the Motherhood of the Virgin Mary.

In the Pauline passage we have heard (cf. Gal 4: 4), the Apostle very discreetly points to the One through whom the Son of God enters the world: Mary of Nazareth, Mother of God, *Theotokos*.

At the beginning of a new year, we are invited, as it were, to attend her school, the school of the faithful disciple of the Lord, in order to learn from her to accept in faith and prayer the salvation God desires to pour out upon those who trust in his merciful love. . . .

"*And Mary kept all these things, reflecting on them in her heart*" (Lk 2: 19).

The first day of the year is placed under the sign of a woman, Mary. The Evangelist Luke describes her as the silent Virgin who listens constantly to the eternal Word, who lives in the Word of God. Mary treasures in her heart the words that come from God and, piecing them together as in a mosaic, learns to understand them.

Let us too, at her school, learn to become attentive and docile disciples of the Lord. With her motherly help, let us commit ourselves to working enthusiastically in the 'workshop' of peace, following Christ, the Prince of Peace.

After the example of the Blessed Virgin, may we let ourselves be guided always and only by Jesus Christ, who is the same yesterday, today, and for ever! (Heb 13: 8). Amen.

APOSTOLIC JOURNEY OF HIS HOLINESS
BENEDICT XVI TO TURKEY
28 NOVEMBER – 1 DECEMBER 2006

From the Homily given at

MASS BEFORE THE SHRINE OF MERYEM ANA EVÌ

Ephesus, Wednesday 29 November 2006

In this Eucharistic celebration we praise the Lord for Mary's divine motherhood, a mystery solemnly confessed and proclaimed in Ephesus at the Ecumenical Council of 431. To this place, so dear to the Christian community, my venerable Predecessors the Servants of God Paul VI and John Paul II came as pilgrims; the latter visited this Shrine on 30 November 1979, just over a year after the beginning of his Pontificate. Another of my Predecessors was in this country not as Pope, but as the Papal Representative, from January 1935 to December 1944, Blessed John XXIII, Angelo Roncalli, whose memory still enkindles great devotion and affection. . . .

Mother of God – Mother of the Church

We have listened to a passage from Saint John's Gospel which invites us to contemplate the moment of the Redemption when Mary, united to her Son in the offering of his sacrifice, extended her motherhood to all men and women, and in particular to the disciples of Jesus. A privileged witness to that event was the author of the Fourth Gospel, John, the only one of the

Apostles to remain at Golgotha with the Mother of Jesus and the other women. Mary's motherhood, which began with her *fiat* in Nazareth, is fulfilled at the foot of the Cross. Although it is true – as Saint Anselm says – that "from the moment of her *fiat* Mary began to carry all of us in her womb", the maternal vocation and mission of the Virgin towards those who believe in Christ actually began when Jesus said to her: "Woman, behold your son!" (Jn 19:26). Looking down from the Cross at his Mother and the beloved disciple by her side, the dying Christ recognized the firstfruits of the family which he had come to form in the world, the beginning of the Church and the new humanity. For this reason, he addressed Mary as "Woman", not as "Mother", the term which he was to use in entrusting her to his disciple: "Behold your Mother!" (Jn 19:27). The Son of God thus fulfilled his mission: born of the Virgin in order to share our human condition in everything but sin, at his return to the Father he left behind in the world the sacrament of the unity of the human race (cf. *Lumen Gentium*, n.1): the family "brought into unity from the unity of the Father and the Son and the Holy Spirit" (Saint Cyprian, *De Orat. Dom.*, 23: *PL* 4, 536), at whose heart is this new bond between the Mother and the disciple. Mary's *divine motherhood* and her *ecclesial motherhood* are thus inseparably united.

Mother of God – Mother of Unity

The first reading presented what could be called the 'Gospel' of the Apostle of the Gentiles: all men and women, including the pagans, are called in Christ to share fully in the mystery of salvation. The text also contains the expression that I have chosen as the motto for my Apostolic Journey: "He, Christ, is our peace" (Eph 2:14). Inspired by the Holy Spirit, Paul tells us that Jesus Christ has not only brought us peace, but that he *is* our peace. And he justifies this statement by referring to the mystery of the Cross: by shedding "his blood", by offering in sacrifice "his flesh", Jesus destroyed hostility "in himself" and created "in himself one new man in place of the two" (Eph 2:14-16). The Apostle explains how, in a truly unforeseen way, messianic peace has now come about in Christ's own person and his saving mystery. He explains it by writing, during his imprisonment, to the Christian community which lived here, in Ephesus: "to the saints who are in Ephesus and are faithful in Christ Jesus" (Eph 1:1), as he says in the salutation of the Letter. The Apostle wishes them "grace and peace from God our Father and the Lord Jesus Christ" (Eph 1:2). *Grace* is the power that transforms man and the world; *peace* is the mature fruit of this transformation. Christ is grace; Christ is peace. Paul knows that he has been sent to proclaim a "mystery", a divine plan that only in the fullness of time has been carried out and revealed in Christ: namely, that "the Gentiles have become fellow heirs, members of the same body, and sharers in the promise in Christ Jesus through the Gospel" (Eph 3:6). This *mystery* is accomplished, in salvation history, *in the Church*, the new People in which, now that the old dividing wall has been broken down, Jews and pagans find themselves united. Like Christ himself, the Church is not only the *instrument* of unity, but also its *efficacious sign*. And the Virgin Mary, the Mother of Christ and of the Church, is the *Mother* of that *mystery of unity* which Christ and the Church inseparably signify and build up, in the world and throughout history.

Magnificat

In today's liturgy we have repeated, as the refrain of the Responsorial Psalm, the song of praise proclaimed by the Virgin of Nazareth on meeting her elderly kinswoman Elizabeth (cf. Lk 1:39). Our hearts too were consoled by the words of the Psalmist: "steadfast love and faithfulness will meet, righteousness and peace will kiss" (Ps 85:10). Dear brothers and sisters, in this visit I have wanted to convey my personal love and spiritual closeness, together with that of the universal Church, to the Christian community here in Turkey, a small minority which faces many challenges and difficulties daily. With firm trust let us sing, together with Mary, a *magnificat* of praise and thanksgiving to God who has looked with favour upon the lowliness of his servant (cf. Lk 1:48). Let us sing joyfully, even when we are tested by difficulties and dangers, as we have learned from the fine witness given by the Roman priest Don Andrea Santoro,* whom I am pleased to recall in this celebration. Mary teaches us that the source of our joy and our one sure support is Christ, and she repeats his words: "Do not be afraid" (Mk 6:50), "I am with you" (Mt 28:20). Mary, Mother of the Church, accompany us always on our way! Holy Mary, Mother of God, pray for us! *Aziz Meryem Mesih'in Annesi bizim için Dua et.* Amen.

* Fr Andrea Santoro was a priest of the Diocese of Rome who had offered to work amongst the Catholic community in Trabzon, Turkey. On 6 February 2006 he was shot dead at the church of Santa Maria, Trabzon, whilst kneeling in prayer, by a sixteen-year old man.

From the Homily given on the

SOLEMNITY OF MARY, MOTHER OF GOD AND 40TH WORLD DAY OF PEACE

St Peter's Basilica
Monday, 1 January 2007

As in a mosaic, today's liturgy contemplates different events and messianic situations, but attention is especially focused on *Mary, Mother of God.* Eight days after Jesus' birth, we commemorate the Mother, the *Theotokos,* the one who gave birth to the Child who is King of Heaven and earth for ever (cf. Entrance Antiphon; Sedulius).*

The liturgy today meditates on the Word made man and repeats that he is born of the Virgin. It reflects on the circumcision of Jesus as a rite of admission to the community and contemplates God who, by means of Mary, gave his Only-Begotten Son to lead the "new people". It recalls the name given to the Messiah and listens to it spoken with tender sweetness by his Mother. It invokes peace for the world, Christ's peace, and does so through

---

*The Entrance Antiphon of the Solemnity being 'Salve, sancta parens,' the antiphon itself being by the early fifth-century Christian poet, Sedulius – 'Hail, holy Mother, thou who didst bring forth the King Who rules Heaven and earth for ever and ever. (*Ps. 44: 2*) My heart hath uttered a good word : I speak my works to the King. Glory be to the Father and to the Son and to the Holy Ghost, as it was in the beginning, is now and ever shall be, world without end. Amen.'

Mary, Mediatrix and Cooperator of Christ (cf. *Lumen Gentium,* nn. 60-61).

We are beginning *a new solar year* which is a further period of time offered to us by divine Providence in the context of the salvation inaugurated by Christ. But did not the eternal Word enter time precisely through Mary? In the Second Reading we have just listened to, the Apostle Paul recalls this by saying that Jesus was born "of woman" (Gal 4: 4).

In today's liturgy *the figure of Mary,* true Mother of Jesus, God-man, *stands out*. Thus, today's Solemnity is not celebrating an abstract idea but a mystery and an historic event: Jesus Christ, a divine Person, is born of the Virgin Mary who is his Mother in the truest sense.

Today too, *Mary's virginity* is highlighted, in addition to her motherhood. These are two prerogatives that are always proclaimed together, inseparably, because they complement and qualify each other. Mary is Mother, but a Virgin Mother; Mary is a virgin, but a Mother Virgin. If either of these aspects is ignored, the mystery of Mary as the Gospels present her to us, cannot be properly understood.

As Mother of Christ, Mary is also *Mother of the Church,* which my venerable Predecessor, the Servant of God Paul VI chose to proclaim on 21 November 1964 at the Second Vatican Council. Lastly, Mary is the *Spiritual Mother of all humanity*, because Jesus on the Cross shed his blood for all of us and from the Cross he entrusted us all to her maternal care.

Let us begin this new year, therefore, by looking at Mary whom we received from God's hands as a precious 'talent' to be made fruitful, a providential opportunity to contribute to bringing about the Kingdom of God. . . .

From the Homily given on the

SOLEMNITY OF MARY, MOTHER OF GOD AND 41ST WORLD DAY OF PEACE

St Peter's Basilica
Tuesday, 1 January 2008

Today, we are beginning a new year and Christian hope takes us by the hand; let us begin it by invoking divine Blessings upon it and imploring, through the intercession of Mary, Mother of God, the gift of peace: for our families, for our cities, for the whole world. . . .

Our thoughts now turn spontaneously to Our Lady, whom we invoke today as the Mother of God. It was Pope Paul VI who moved to 1 January the Feast of the Divine Motherhood of Mary, which was formerly celebrated on 11 October. Indeed, even before the liturgical reform that followed the Second Vatican Council, the memorial of the circumcision of Jesus on the eighth day after his birth – as a sign of submission to the law, his official insertion in the Chosen People – used to be celebrated on the first day of the year and the Feast of the Name of Jesus was celebrated the following Sunday. We perceive a few traces of these celebrations in the Gospel passage that has just been proclaimed, in which St Luke says that eight days after his birth the Child was circumcised and was given the name "Jesus", "the name given by the Angel before he was conceived in [his

Mother's] . . . womb" (Lk 2: 21). Today's feast, therefore, as well as being a particularly significant Marian feast, also preserves a strongly Christological content because, we might say, before the Mother, it concerns the Son, Jesus, true God and true Man.

The Apostle Paul refers to the mystery of the divine motherhood of Mary, the *Theotokos,* in his Letter to the Galatians. "When the time had fully come", he writes, "God sent forth his Son, born of woman, born under the law" (4: 4). We find the mystery of the Incarnation of the Divine Word and the Divine Motherhood of Mary summed up in a few words: the Virgin's great privilege is precisely to be Mother of the Son who is God. The most logical and proper place for this Marian feast is therefore eight days after Christmas. Indeed, in the night of Bethlehem, when "she gave birth to her first-born son" (Lk 2: 7), the prophesies concerning the Messiah were fulfilled. "The virgin shall be with child and bear a son", Isaiah had foretold (7: 14); "Behold, you will conceive in your womb and bear a son", the Angel Gabriel said to Mary (Lk 1: 31); and again, an Angel of the Lord, the Evangelist Matthew recounts, appeared to Joseph in a dream to reassure him and said: "Do not fear to take Mary for your wife, for that which is conceived in her is of the Holy Spirit; she will bear a son" (Mt 1: 20-21).

The title 'Mother of God', together with the title 'Blessed Virgin', is the oldest on which all the other titles with which Our Lady was venerated are based, and it continues to be invoked from generation to generation in the East and in the West. A multitude of hymns and a wealth of prayers of the Christian tradition refer to the mystery of her divine motherhood, such as, for example, a Marian antiphon of the Christmas season, *Alma Redemptoris mater*, with which we pray in these words: "*Tu quae genuisti, natura mirante, tuum sanctum Genitorem, Virgo prius ac posterius* – You, in the wonder of all creation, have brought forth your Creator, Mother ever virgin". Dear brothers and sisters, let us today contemplate Mary, ever-virgin Mother of the Only-Begotten Son of the Father; let us learn from her to welcome the Child who was born for us in Bethlehem. If we recognize in the Child born of her the Eternal Son of God and accept him as our one Saviour, we can be called and we really are children of God: sons in the Son. The Apostle writes: "God sent forth his Son, born of woman, born under the law, to redeem those who were under the law, so that we might receive adoption as sons" (Gal 4: 4).

The Evangelist Luke repeats several times that Our Lady meditated silently on these extraordinary events in which God had involved her. We also heard this in the short Gospel passage that the Liturgy presents to us today. "Mary kept all these things, pondering them in her heart" (Lk 2: 19).

The Greek verb used, *sumbállousa,* literally means 'piecing together' and makes us think of a great mystery to be discovered little by little. Although the Child lying in a manger looks like all children in the world, at the same time he is totally different: he is the Son of God, he is God, true God and true man. This mystery – the Incarnation of the Word and the divine Motherhood of Mary – is great and certainly far from easy to understand with the human mind alone.

Yet, by learning from Mary, we can understand with our hearts what our eyes and minds do not manage to perceive or contain on their own. Indeed, this is such a great gift that only through faith are we granted to accept it, while not entirely understanding it. And it is precisely on this journey of faith that Mary comes to meet us as our support and guide. She is mother because she brought forth Jesus in the flesh; she is mother because she adhered totally to the Father's will. St Augustine wrote: "The divine motherhood would have been of no value to her had she not borne Christ in her heart, with a destiny more fortunate than the moment when she conceived him in the flesh" (*De*

Sancta Virginitate, 3, 3). And in her heart Mary continued to treasure, to 'piece together' the subsequent events of which she was to be a witness and protagonist, even to the death on the Cross and the Resurrection of her Son Jesus.

Dear brothers and sisters, it is only by pondering in the heart, in other words, by piecing together and finding unity in all we experience, that, following Mary, we can penetrate the mystery of a God who was made man out of love and who calls us to follow him on the path of love; a love to be expressed daily by generous service to the brethren. May the new year which we are confidently beginning today be a time in which to advance in that knowledge of the heart, which is the wisdom of saints. Let us pray, as we heard in the First Reading, that the Lord may "make his face to shine" upon us, "and be gracious" to us (cf. Nm 6: 24-7) and bless us. We may be certain of it: if we never tire of seeking his Face, if we never give in to the temptation of discouragement and doubt, if also among the many difficulties we encounter we always remain anchored to him, we will experience the power of his love and his mercy. May the fragile Child who today the Virgin shows to the world make us peacemakers, witnesses of him, the Prince of Peace. Amen!

GENERAL AUDIENCE

Paul VI Audience Hall
Wednesday, 2 January 2008

Mary, Mother of God

Yesterday, we celebrated the solemn Feast of Mary, Mother of God. 'Mother of God', *Theotokos,* is the title that was officially attributed to Mary in the fifth century, to be exact, at the Council of Ephesus in 431, but which had already taken root in the devotion of the Christian people since the third century, in the context of the heated discussions on the Person of Christ in that period. This title highlights the fact that Christ is God and truly was born of Mary as a man: in this way his unity as true God and true man is preserved. Actually, however much the debate might seem to focus on Mary, it essentially concerned the Son. Desiring to safeguard the full humanity of Jesus, several Fathers suggested a weaker term: instead of the title *Theotokos,* they suggested *Christotokos,* 'Mother of Christ'; however, this was rightly seen as a threat to the doctrine of the full unity of Christ's divinity with his humanity. On the one hand, therefore, after lengthy discussion at the Council of Ephesus in 431, as I said, the unity of the two natures – the divine and the human (cf. *DS*, n. 250) – in the Person of the Son of God was solemnly confirmed and, on the other, the legitimacy of the attribution of the title *Theotokos,* Mother of God, to the Virgin (ibid., n. 251).

After this Council a true explosion of Marian devotion was recorded and many churches dedicated to the Mother of God were built. Outstanding among these is the Basilica of St Mary

Major here in Rome. The teaching on Mary, Mother of God, received further confirmation at the Council of Chalcedon (451), at which Christ was declared "true God and true man . . . born for us and for our salvation of Mary, Virgin and Mother of God, in his humanity" (*DS*, n. 301). As is well known, the Second Vatican Council gathered the teachings on Mary in the eighth chapter of the Dogmatic Constitution on the Church *Lumen Gentium*, reaffirming her divine motherhood. The chapter is entitled "The Blessed Virgin Mary, Mother of God, in the Mystery of Christ and the Church".

Thus, the description 'Mother of God', so deeply bound up with the Christmas festivities, is therefore the fundamental name with which the Community of Believers has always honoured the Blessed Virgin. It clearly explains Mary's mission in salvation history. All other titles attributed to Our Lady are based on her vocation to be the Mother of the Redeemer, the human creature chosen by God to bring about the plan of salvation, centred on the great mystery of the Incarnation of the Divine Word. In these days of festivity we have paused to contemplate the depiction of the Nativity in the crib. At the centre of this scene we find the Virgin Mother, who offers the Baby Jesus for the contemplation of all those who come to adore the Saviour: the shepherds, the poor people of Bethlehem, the Magi from the East. Later, on the Feast of the Presentation which we celebrate on 2 February, it will be the elderly Simeon and the prophetess Anna who receive the tiny Infant from the hands of his Mother and worship him. The devotion of the Christian people has always considered the Birth of Jesus and the divine motherhood of Mary as two aspects of the same mystery of the Incarnation of the Divine Word, so it has never thought of the Nativity as a thing of the past. We are 'contemporaries' of the shepherds, the Magi, of Simeon and of Anna, and as we go with them we are filled with joy, because God wanted to be the God-with-us and has a mother who is our mother.

All the other titles with which the Church honours Our Lady then derive from the title 'Mother of God', but this one is fundamental. Let us think of the privilege of the 'Immaculate Conception', that is, of Mary being immune to sin from conception: she was preserved from any stain of sin because she was to be the Mother of the Redeemer. The same applies to the title 'Our Lady of the Assumption': the One who had brought forth the Saviour could not be subject to the corruption that derives from original sin. And we know that all these privileges were not granted in order to distance Mary from us but, on the contrary, to bring her close; indeed, since she was totally with God, this woman is very close to us and helps us as a mother and a sister. The unique and unrepeatable position that Mary occupies in the Community of Believers also stems from her fundamental vocation to being Mother of the Redeemer. Precisely as such, Mary is also Mother of the Mystical Body of Christ, which is the Church. Rightly, therefore, on 21 November 1964 during the Second Vatican Council, Paul VI solemnly attributed to Mary the title 'Mother of the Church'.

It is because she is Mother of the Church that the Virgin is also the Mother of each one of us, members of the Mystical Body of Christ. From the Cross, Jesus entrusted his Mother to all his disciples and at the same time entrusted all his disciples to the love of his Mother. The Evangelist John concludes the brief and evocative account with these words: "Then he said to the disciple, 'Behold, your mother!' And from that hour the disciple took her to his own home" (Jn 19: 27). This is the [English] translation of the Greek text "εἰς τά ἴδια", he welcomed her into his own reality, his own existence. Thus, she is part of his life and the two lives penetrate each other. And this acceptance of her (εἰς τά ἴδια) in his own life is the Lord's testament. Therefore, at the supreme moment of the fulfilment of his messianic mission, Jesus bequeathes as a precious inheritance to each one of his disciples his own Mother, the Virgin Mary.

Dear brothers and sisters, in these first days of the year, we are invited to consider attentively the importance of Mary's presence in the life of the Church and in our own lives. Let us entrust ourselves to her so that she may guide our steps in this new period of time which the Lord gives us to live, and help us to be authentic friends of his Son and thus also courageous builders of his Kingdom in the world, a Kingdom of light and truth.. . . May the new year, which began under the sign of the Virgin Mary, bring us a deeper awareness of her motherly presence so that, sustained and comforted by the Virgin's protection, we may contemplate the Face of her Son Jesus with new eyes and walk more quickly on the paths of good.

From the Homily given at the

TE DEUM AND FIRST VESPERS OF THE SOLEMNITY OF MARY, MOTHER OF GOD

St Peter's Basilica
Wednesday, 31 December 2008

The year that is ending and that which is approaching on the horizon are both under the blessed gaze of the Most Holy Mother of God. The artistic polychrome sculpture set here next to the altar, which portrays her on a throne with the Child giving his Blessing, also recalls her motherly presence. We are celebrating the First Vespers of this Marian Solemnity, in which there are numerous liturgical references to the mystery of the Virgin's divine motherhood.

"*O admirabile commercium!* O marvelous exchange!" Thus begins the Antiphon of the first Psalm, to then continue: "man's Creator has become man, born of a virgin". "By your miraculous birth of the Virgin you have fulfilled the Scriptures", proclaims the Antiphon of the Second Psalm, which is echoed by the words of the third Antiphon that introduce us to the canticle taken from the Letter of Paul to the Ephesians: "Your blessed and fruitful virginity is like the bush, flaming yet unburned, which Moses saw on Sinai. Pray for us, Mother of God." Mary's divine motherhood is also highlighted in the brief Reading proclaimed shortly beforehand, which proposes anew the well-known verses of the Letter to the Galatians: "When the designated time had come, God sent forth his Son, born of woman . . .

so that we might receive our status as adopted sons" (Gal 4: 4-5). And again, in the traditional *Te Deum* that we will raise at the end of our celebration before the Most Holy Sacrament solemnly exposed for our adoration singing, "*Tu, ad liberandum suscepturus hominem, non horruisti Virginis uterum*", in English: "when you, O Christ, became man to set us free you did not spurn the Virgin's womb."

Thus everything this evening invites us to turn our gaze to the one who "received the Word of God in her heart and in her body and gave Life to the world", and who for this very reason, the Second Vatican Ecumenical Council recalls, "is acknowledged and honoured as being truly the Mother of God" (*Lumen Gentium*, n. 53). Christ's Nativity, which we are commemorating in these days, is entirely suffused with the light of Mary and, while we pause at the manger to contemplate the Child, our gaze cannot fail to turn in gratitude also to his Mother, who with her 'yes' made possible the gift of Redemption. This is why the Christmas Season brings with it a profoundly Marian connotation; the birth of Jesus as God and man and Mary's divine motherhood are inseparable realities; the mystery of Mary and the mystery of the Only-Begotten Son of God who was made man form a single mystery, in which the one helps to better understand the other.

Mary Mother of God, *Theotokos, Dei Genetrix.* Since ancient times Our Lady has been honoured with this title. However, for many centuries in the West there was no feast specifically dedicated to the divine Motherhood of Mary. It was introduced into the Latin Church by Pope Pius XI in 1931 on the occasion of the fifteenth centenary of the Council of Ephesus, and he chose to establish it on 11 October. On that date, in 1962, the Second Vatican Council was inaugurated. It was then the Servant of God Paul VI who restored an ancient tradition in 1969, fixing this Solemnity on 1 January. In the Apostolic

Exhortation *Marialis Cultus* of 2 February 1974, he explained the reason for his decision and its connection with the World Day of Peace. "In the revised ordering of the Christmas period it seems to us that the attention of all should be directed towards the restored Solemnity of Mary the holy Mother of God," Paul VI wrote. "This celebration . . . is meant to commemorate the part played by Mary in this mystery of salvation. It is meant also to exalt the singular dignity which this mystery brings to the 'holy Mother'. . . . It is likewise a fitting occasion for renewing adoration to the newborn Prince of Peace, for listening once more to the glad tidings of the angels (cf. Lk 2: 14), and for imploring from God, through the Queen of Peace, the supreme gift of peace" (n. 5).

Homily of His Holiness Benedict XVI

SOLEMNITY OF MARY, MOTHER OF GOD AND 43RD WORLD DAY OF PEACE

Vatican Basilica
Friday, 1st January 2010

Venerable Brothers, Distinguished Ladies and Gentlemen, Dear Brothers and Sisters,

On the first day of the New Year we have the joy and the grace of celebrating the Most Holy Mother of God and, at the same time, the World Day of Peace. In both these events we are celebrating Christ, Son of God, born of the Virgin Mary and our true peace! To all of you who are gathered here: representatives of the world's peoples, of the Roman and universal Church, priests and faithful; and to all who are connected via radio and television, I repeat the words of the ancient Blessing: "The Lord lift up his countenance upon you, and give you peace" (Nm 6: 26). Today I wish to develop precisely the theme of the Face and of faces, in the light of the word of God the Face of God and human faces a theme that also gives us a key to the interpretation of the problem of peace in the world.

We heard in both the First Reading from the Book of Numbers and in the Responsorial Psalm, several expressions with reference to God that contain the metaphor of the face: "The Lord make his face to shine upon you, / and be gracious to you" (Nm 6: 25).

"May God be gracious to us and bless us /and make his face to shine upon us / that your way may be known upon earth, / your saving power among all nations" (Ps 67[66]: 1-3). The face is the expression of the person par excellence. It is what makes him or her recognizable and from it transpire sentiments, thoughts and heartfelt intentions. God by his nature is invisible, yet the Bible applies this image to him too. Showing his face is an expression of his benevolence, whereas hiding it indicates his anger and indignation. The Book of Exodus says that "The Lord used to speak to Moses face to face, as a man speaks to his friend" (Ex 33: 11), and again it was to Moses that the Lord promised his closeness with a very unusual formula: "my presence [face] will go with you, and I will give you rest" (Ex 33: 14). The Psalms show believers to us as those who seek God's Face (cf. Ps 27[26]: 8); 105[104]: 4), and who, in worship, long to see him (Ps 42[41]: 3) and tell us that "the upright" shall "behold his face" (Ps 11[10]: 7).

One may interpret the whole biblical narrative as the gradual revelation of the Face of God, until it reaches his full manifestation in Jesus Christ. "When the time had fully come", the Apostle Paul has reminded us today too, "God sent forth his Son", (Gal 4: 4), immediately adding, "born of woman, born under the law". God's Face took on a human face, letting itself be seen and recognized in the Son of the Virgin Mary, who for this reason we venerate with the loftiest title of "Mother of God". She, who had preserved in her heart the secret of the divine motherhood, was the first to see the face of God made man in the small fruit of her womb. The Mother had a very special, unique and, in a certain way, exclusive relationship with the newborn Son. The first face a child sees is that of his mother and this gaze is crucial for his relationship with life, with himself, with others and with God; it is also crucial if he is to become a "son of peace" (Lk 10: 6). Among the many typologies of icons of the Virgin Mary in the Byzantine tradition is the one called "of tenderness" that portrays the Child Jesus with his face resting, cheek to cheek, against his Mother's. The Child gazes at the Mother and she is looking at us, almost as if to mirror for those who are observing and praying the tenderness of God who came down to her from Heaven and was incarnate in the Son of man, whom she holds in her arms. We can contemplate in this Marian image something of God himself: a sign of the ineffable love that impelled him "to give his Only Son" (cf. Jn 3: 16). But that same icon also shows us, in Mary, the face of the Church which reflects Christ's light upon us and upon the whole world, the Church through which the Good News reaches every person: "You are no longer a slave but a son" (Gal 4: 7), as once again we read in St Paul.

V

CANA

APOSTOLIC JOURNEY OF HIS HOLINESS BENEDICT XVI TO MUNICH, ALTÖTTING AND REGENSBURG 9-14 SEPTEMBER 2006

From the Homily given during the

HOLY MASS

Kapellplatz, Altötting
Monday, 11 September 2006

In today's First Reading, Responsorial Psalm and Gospel, three times and in three different ways, we see Mary, the Mother of the Lord, as a woman of prayer. In the Book of Acts we find her in the midst of the community of the Apostles gathered in the Upper Room, praying that the Lord, now ascended to the Father, will fulfil his promise: "Within a few days you will be baptized with the Holy Spirit" (1:5). Mary leads the nascent Church in prayer; she is, as it were in person, the Church at prayer. And thus, along with the great community of the saints and at their centre, she stands even today before God interceding for us, asking her Son to send his Spirit once more upon the Church and to renew the face of the earth.

We responded to this reading by singing with Mary the great hymn of praise which she raises after Elizabeth calls her blessed because of her faith. It is a prayer of thanksgiving, of joy in God, of blessing for his mighty works. The tenor of this song is clear from its very first words: "My soul magnifies – makes great – the Lord". Making the Lord great means giving him a place in the world, in our lives, and letting him enter into our time and our activity: ultimately this is the essence of true prayer. Where God is made great, men and women are not made small: there too men and women become great and the world is filled with light.

Finally, in the Gospel passage, Mary makes a request of her Son on behalf of some friends in need. At first sight, this could appear to be an entirely human conversation between a Mother and her Son and it is indeed a dialogue rich in humanity. Yet Mary does not speak to Jesus as if he were a mere man on whose ability and helpfulness she can count. She entrusts a human need to his power – to a power which is more than skill and human ability. In this dialogue with Jesus, we actually see her as a Mother who asks, one who intercedes. As we listen to this Gospel passage, it is worth going a little deeper, not only to understand Jesus and Mary better, but also to learn from Mary the right way to pray. Mary does not really ask something of Jesus: she simply says to him: "They have no wine" (Jn 2:3). Weddings in the Holy Land were celebrated for a whole week; the entire town took part, and consequently much wine was consumed. Now the bride and groom find themselves in trouble, and Mary simply says this to Jesus. She doesn't ask for anything specific, much less that Jesus exercise his power, perform a miracle, produce wine. She simply hands the matter over to Jesus and leaves it to him to decide about what to do. In the simple words of the Mother of Jesus, then, we can see two things: on the one hand her affectionate concern for people, that maternal affection which makes her aware of the problems of others. We see her heartfelt goodness and her willingness to help. This is the Mother that generations of people have come here to Altötting to visit. To her we entrust our cares, our needs and our troubles. Her maternal readiness to help, in which we trust, appears here for the first time in the Holy Scriptures. But in addition to this first aspect, with which we are all familiar, there is another, which we could easily overlook: Mary leaves everything to the Lord's judgement. At Nazareth she gave over her will, immersing it in the will of God: "Here am I, the servant of the Lord; let it be with me according to your word" (Lk 1:38). And this continues to be her fundamental attitude. This is how she teaches us to pray: not by seeking to assert before God our own will and our own desires, however important they may be, however reasonable they might appear to us, but rather to bring them before him and to let him decide what he intends to do. From Mary we learn graciousness and readiness to help, but we also learn humility and generosity in accepting God's will, in the confident conviction that, whatever it may be, it will be our, and my own, true good.

We can understand, I think, very well the attitude and words of Mary, yet we still find it very hard to understand Jesus' answer. In the first place, we don't like the way he addresses her: "Woman". Why doesn't he say: "Mother"? But this title really expresses Mary's place in salvation history. It points to the future, to the hour of the crucifixion, when Jesus will say to her: "Woman, behold your son – Son, behold your mother" (cf. Jn 19:26-27). It anticipates the hour when he will make the woman, his Mother, the Mother of all his disciples. On the other hand, the title "Woman" recalls the account of the creation of Eve: Adam, surrounded by creation in all its magnificence, experiences loneliness as a human being. Then Eve is created, and in her Adam finds the companion whom he longed for; and he gives her the name "woman". In the Gospel of John, then, Mary represents the new, the definitive woman, the companion of the Redeemer, our Mother: the name, which seemed so lacking in affection, actually expresses the grandeur of Mary's enduring mission.

Yet we like even less what Jesus at Cana then says to Mary: "Woman, what have I to do with you? My hour has not yet come" (Jn 2:4). We want to object: you have a lot to do with her! It was Mary who gave you flesh and blood, who gave you your body, and not only your body: with the 'yes' which rose from the depths of her heart she bore you in her womb and with a mother's love she gave you life and introduced you to the community of the people of Israel. But if this is how we speak to Jesus, then we are already well along the way towards understanding his answer. Because all this should remind us that at the Incarnation of Jesus two dialogues took place; the two go together and blend into one. First, there is Mary's dialogue with the Archangel Gabriel, where she says: "Let it be with me according to your word" (Lk 1:38). But there is a text parallel to this, so to speak, within God himself, which we read about in the Letter to the Hebrews, when it says that the words of Psalm 40 became a kind of dialogue between the Father and the Son – a dialogue which set in motion the Incarnation. The Eternal Son says to the Father: "Sacrifices and offerings you have not desired, but a body you have prepared for me. . . . See, I have come to do your will" (Heb 10:5-7; cf. Ps 40:6-8). The 'yes' of the Son: "I have come to do your will", and the 'yes' of Mary: "Let it be with me according to your word" – this double 'yes' – becomes a single 'yes', and thus the Word becomes flesh in Mary. In this double 'yes' the obedience of the Son is embodied, and by her own 'yes' Mary gives him that body. "Woman, what have I to do with you?" Ultimately, what each has to do with the other is found in this double 'yes' which resulted in the Incarnation. The Lord's answer points to this point of profound unity. It is precisely to this that he points his Mother. Here, in their common 'yes' to the will of the Father, an answer is found. We too need to learn always anew how to progress towards this point; there we will find the answer to our questions.

If we take this as our starting-point, we can now also understand the second part of Jesus' answer: "My hour has not yet come". Jesus never acts completely alone, and never for the sake of pleasing others. The Father is always the starting-point of his actions, and this is what unites him to Mary, because she wished to make her request in this same unity of will with the Father. And so, surprisingly, after hearing Jesus' answer, which apparently refuses her request, she can simply say to the servants: "Do whatever he tells you" (Jn 2:5). Jesus is not a wonder-worker, he does not play games with his power in what is, after all, a private affair. No, he gives a sign, in which he proclaims his hour, the hour of the wedding-feast, the hour of union between God and man. He does not merely 'make' wine, but transforms the human wedding-feast into an image of the divine wedding-feast, to which the Father invites us through the Son and in which he gives us every good thing, represented by the abundance of wine. The wedding-feast becomes an image of that moment when Jesus pushed love to the utmost, let his body be rent and thus gave himself to us for ever, having become completely one with us – a marriage between God and man. The hour of the Cross, the hour which is the source of the Sacrament, in which he gives himself really to us in flesh and blood, puts his Body into our hands and our hearts, this is the hour of the wedding feast. Thus a momentary need is resolved in a truly divine manner and the initial request is superabundantly granted. Jesus' hour has not yet arrived, but in the sign of the water changed into wine, in the sign of the festive gift, he even now anticipates that hour.

Jesus' 'hour' is the Cross; his definitive hour will be his return at the end of time. He continually anticipates also this definitive hour in the Eucharist, in which, even now, he always comes to us. And he does this ever anew through the intercession of his Mother, through the intercession of the Church, which cries out to him in the Eucharistic prayers: "Come, Lord Jesus!" In the Canon of the Mass, the Church constantly prays for this 'hour' to be anticipated, asking that he may come even now and be given to us. And so we want to let ourselves be guided by Mary, by the Mother of Graces of Altötting, by the Mother of all the faithful, towards the 'hour' of Jesus. Let us ask him for the gift of a deeper knowledge and understanding of him. And may our reception of him not be reduced to the moment of Communion alone. Jesus remains present in the sacred Host and he awaits us constantly. Here in Altötting, the adoration of the Lord in the Eucharist has found a new location in the old treasury. Mary and Jesus go together. Through Mary we want to continue our conversing with the Lord and to learn how to receive him better. Holy Mother of God, pray for us, just as at Cana you prayed for the bride and the bridegroom! Guide us towards Jesus – ever anew! Amen!

VI
STABAT MATER

WAY OF THE CROSS
AT THE COLOSSEUM

From the

MEDITATIONS AND PRAYERS BY CARDINAL JOSEPH RATZINGER

Good Friday 2005

From the Gospel according to Luke. 2:34-35,51

Simon blessed them and said to Mary his mother: "Behold, this child is set for the fall and rising of many in Israel, and for a sign that is spoken against (and a sword will pierce through your own soul also), that thoughts out of many hearts may be revealed." And his mother kept all these things in her heart.

Meditation

On Jesus' Way of the Cross, we also find Mary, his Mother. During his public life she had to step aside, to make space for the birth of Jesus' new family, the family of his disciples. She also had to hear the words: "Who is my mother and who are my brothers? . . . Whoever does the will of my Father in heaven is brother, and sister and mother" (Mt 12:48-50). Now we see her as the Mother of Jesus, not only physically, but also in her heart. Even before she conceived him bodily, through her obedience she conceived him in her heart. It was said to Mary: "And behold, you will conceive in your womb and bear a son.

He will be great and the Lord God will give to him the throne of his father David" (Lk 1:31ff.). And she would hear from the mouth of the elderly Simeon: "A sword will pierce through your own soul" (Lk 2:35). She would then recall the words of the prophets, words like these: "He was oppressed, and he was afflicted, yet he opened not his mouth; he was like a lamb that is led to slaughter" (Is 54:7). Now it all takes place. In her heart she had kept the words of the Angel, spoken to her in the beginning: "Do not be afraid, Mary" (Lk 1:30). The disciples fled, yet she did not flee. She stayed there, with a Mother's courage, a Mother's fidelity, a Mother's goodness, and a faith which did not waver in the hour of darkness: "Blessed is she who believed" (Lk 1:45). "Nevertheless, when the Son of man comes, will he find faith on earth?" (Lk 18:8). Yes, in this moment Jesus knows: he will find faith. In this hour, this is his great consolation.

Prayer

Holy Mary, Mother of the Lord, you remained faithful when the disciples fled. Just as you believed the Angel's incredible message – that you would become the Mother of the Most High – so too you believed at the hour of his greatest abasement. In this way, at the hour of the Cross, at the hour of the world's darkest night, you became the Mother of all believers, the Mother of the Church. We beg you: teach us to believe, and grant that our faith may bear fruit in courageous service and be the sign of a love ever ready to share suffering and to offer assistance.

GENERAL AUDIENCE

Papal Summer Residence, Castel Gandolfo
Wednesday, 12 August 2009

Connection between the Blessed Virgin Mary and the priesthood

Dear Brothers and Sisters,

The celebration of the Solemnity of the Assumption of the Blessed Virgin Mary, next Saturday, is at hand and we are in the context of the Year for Priests. I therefore wish to speak of the link between Our Lady and the priesthood. This connection is deeply rooted in the Mystery of the Incarnation.

When God decided to become man in his Son, he needed the freely-spoken 'yes' of one of his creatures. God does not act against our freedom. And something truly extraordinary happens: God makes himself dependent on the free decision, the 'yes' of one of his creatures; he waits for this 'yes'. St Bernard of Clairvaux explained dramatically in one of his homilies this crucial moment in universal history when Heaven, earth and God himself wait for what this creature will say.

Mary's 'yes' is therefore the door through which God was able to enter the world, to become man. So it is that Mary is truly and profoundly involved in the Mystery of the Incarnation, of our salvation. And the Incarnation, the Son's becoming man, was the beginning that prepared the ground for the gift of himself; for giving himself with great love on the Cross to become Bread for the life of the world. Hence sacrifice, priesthood and Incarnation go together and Mary is at the heart of this mystery.

Let us now go to the Cross. Before dying, Jesus sees his Mother beneath the Cross and he sees the beloved son. This beloved son is certainly a person, a very important individual, but he is more; he is an example, a prefiguration of all beloved disciples, of all the people called by the Lord to be the "beloved disciple" and thus also particularly of priests. Jesus says to Mary: "Woman, behold, your son!" (Jn 19: 26). It is a sort of testament: he entrusts his Mother to the care of the son, of the disciple. But he also says to the disciple: "Behold, your mother!" (Jn 19: 27). The Gospel tells us that from that hour St John, the beloved son, took his mother Mary "to his own home". This is what it says in the [English] translation; but the Greek text is far deeper, far richer. We could translate it: he took Mary into his inner life, his inner being, "εἰς τὰ ἴδια", into the depths of his being. To take Mary with one means to introduce her into the dynamism of one's own entire existence – it is not something external – and into all that constitutes the horizon of one's own apostolate. It seems to me that one can, therefore, understand how the special relationship of motherhood that exists between Mary and priests may constitute the primary source, the fundamental reason for her special love for each one of them. In fact, Mary loves them with predilection for two reasons: because they are more like Jesus, the supreme love of her heart, and because, like her, they are committed to the mission of proclaiming, bearing witness to and giving Christ to the world. Because of his identification with and sacramental conformation to Jesus, Son of God and Son of Mary, every priest can and must feel that he really is a specially beloved son of this loftiest and humblest of Mothers.

The Second Vatican Council invites priests to look to Mary as to the perfect model for their existence, invoking her as "Mother of the supreme and eternal Priest, as Queen of Apostles, and as Protectress of their ministry". The Council continues, "priests should always venerate and love her, with a filial devotion and worship" (cf. *Presbyterorum Ordinis,* n. 18). The Holy Curé d'Ars, whom we are remembering in particular in this Year, used to like to say: "Jesus Christ, after giving us all that he could give us, wanted further to make us heirs to his most precious possession, that is, his Holy Mother." This applies for every Christian, for all of us, but in a special way for priests. Dear brothers and sisters, let us pray that Mary will make all priests, in all the problems of today's world, conform with the image of her Son Jesus, as stewards of the precious treasure of his love as the Good Shepherd. Mary, Mother of priests, pray for us!

VII
REGINA CAELI, LAETARE

REGINA CAELI

Courtyard of the Papal Residence, Castel Gandolfo
Easter Monday, 24 March 2008

At the solemn Easter Vigil after the days of Lent the singing of the "Alleluia", a Hebrew word known across the world that means "Praise the Lord", rings out once again. During the days of Eastertide this invitation spreads by word of mouth, from heart to heart. It re-echoes an absolutely new event: Christ's death and Resurrection. The "alleluia" welled up in the hearts of Jesus' first disciples, men and women, on that Easter morning in Jerusalem. . . . It almost seems as though we hear their voices: that of Mary of Magdala, who was the first to see the Risen Lord in the garden near Calvary; the voices of the women who met him as they ran, fearful but happy, to tell the disciples the news of the empty tomb; the voices of the two disciples who had set out for Emmaus with gloomy faces and returned to Jerusalem in the evening, filled with joy at having heard his words and recognized him "in the breaking of the bread"; the voices of the Eleven Apostles who on that same evening saw the Lord appearing in their midst in the Upper Room, showing them the wounds of the nails and spear and saying to them: "Peace be with you". This experience engraved the "alleluia" in the Church's heart once and for all!

From this experience too stems the *Regina Caeli*, the prayer that we recite instead of the Angelus today and every day in the Easter Season. The text that replaces the Angelus in these weeks is brief and has the direct form of an announcement: it is like a new 'Annunciation' to Mary, this time not made by an Angel but by us Christians who invite the Mother to rejoice because her Son, whom she carried in her womb, is risen as he promised. Indeed, "rejoice" was the first word that the heavenly messenger addressed to the Virgin in Nazareth. And this is what it meant: Rejoice, Mary, because the Son of God is about to become man within you. Now, after the drama of the Passion, a new invitation to rejoice rings out: *"Gaude et laetare, Virgo Maria, alleluia, quia surrexit Dominus vere, alleluia* – "Rejoice and be glad, O Virgin Mary, alleluia. Rejoice because the Lord is truly risen, alleluia!"

Dear brothers and sisters, let us allow the paschal "alleluia" to be deeply impressed within us too, so that it is not only a word in certain external circumstances but is expressed in our own lives, the lives of people who invite everyone to praise the Lord and do so with their behaviour as "risen" ones. "Pray the Lord for us", we say to Mary, that the One who restored joy to the whole world by means of his Son's Resurrection may grant us to enjoy such gladness now and always, in our life and in the life without end.

From the

REGINA CAELI

St Peter's Square
Seventh Sunday of Easter, 4 May 2008

In his farewell discourses to the disciples, Jesus stressed the importance of his "return to the Father", the culmination of his whole mission: indeed, he came into the world to bring man back to God, not on the ideal level – like a philosopher or a master of wisdom – but really, like a shepherd who wants to lead his sheep back to the fold. This 'exodus' toward the heavenly Homeland which Jesus lived in the first person, he faced solely for us. It was for our sake that he came down from Heaven and for our sake that he ascended to it, after making himself in all things like men, humbling himself even to death on a cross and after having touched the abyss of the greatest distance from God. For this very reason the Father was pleased with him and "highly exalted" him (Phil 2: 9), restoring to him the fullness of his glory, but now with our humanity. God in man – man in God: this is even now a reality, not a theoretical truth. Therefore, Christian hope, founded on Christ, is not an illusion but, as the Letter to the Hebrews says, "we have this as a sure and steadfast anchor of the soul" (Heb 6: 19), an anchor that penetrates Heaven where Christ has gone before us.

And what does the human person in every epoch need other than this: a firm anchorage in life? Here once again is the wonderful meaning of Mary's presence among us. Turning our gaze to her, like the first disciples, we are immediately directed to the reality of Jesus: the Mother points to the Son who is no longer physically among us but awaits us in the Father's house. Jesus invites us not to linger looking upwards, but to be united in prayer together, to invoke the gift of the Holy Spirit. Indeed, only those who are "born from on high", that is, from God's Spirit, have access to the Kingdom of Heaven (cf. Jn 3: 3-5), and the first to be "born from on high" was, precisely, the Virgin Mary. To her, therefore, let us turn in the fullness of Easter joy.

ADDRESS OF HIS HOLINESS BENEDICT XVI

Marian Vigil for the conclusion of the month of May, Vatican Gardens
Saturday, 30 May 2009

I greet you all with affection at the end of the traditional Marian Vigil that concludes the month of May in the Vatican. This year it has acquired a quite special value because it occurs on the eve of Pentecost. In gathering together in spiritual recollection around the Virgin Mary and contemplating the mysteries of the Holy Rosary, you have relived the experience of the first disciples, who gathered in the Upper Room together with "the Mother of Jesus" and "with one accord devoted . . . to prayer", awaited the coming of the Holy Spirit (cf. Acts 1:14). Let us too, on this penultimate evening of May, pray for the outpouring of the Spirit Paraclete upon us, upon the Church in Rome and upon the entire Christian People.

The great Feast of Pentecost invites us to meditate on the relationship between the Holy Spirit and Mary, a very close, privileged and indissoluble relationship. The Virgin of Nazareth was chosen in advance to become the Mother of the Redeemer through the power of the Holy Spirit: in her humility, she found favour in God's eyes (cf. Lk 1:30). In fact, in the New Testament we see that Mary's faith, so to speak, 'attracts' the gift of the Holy Spirit. First of all in the conception of the Son of God, a mystery that the Archangel Gabriel himself explains in this way: "The Holy Spirit will come upon you, and the power of the Most High will overshadow you" (Lk 1:35). Immediately afterwards

Mary went to help Elizabeth, and when she arrived and greeted her, the Holy Spirit caused the child to leap in the womb of her elderly kinswoman (cf. Lk 1:44); and the whole dialogue between the two mothers is inspired by God's Spirit, especially the *Magnificat,* the hymn of praise in which Mary expresses her innermost sentiments. The whole event of Jesus' birth and early childhood is guided almost tangibly by the Holy Spirit, although he is not always mentioned. Mary's heart, in perfect unison with the divine Son, is a temple of the Spirit of truth in which every word and every event are preserved in faith, hope and charity (cf. Lk 2:19, 51).

We may therefore be certain that the most Sacred Heart of Jesus, in the whole of his hidden life in Nazareth always found in his Mother's Immaculate Heart, a 'hearth' ever alight with prayer and with constant attention to the voice of the Spirit. The events at the Wedding at Cana are an attestation of this unique harmony between the Mother and the Son in seeking God's will. In a situation laden with symbols of the Covenant, such as the wedding feast, the Virgin Mother intercedes and provokes, so to speak, a sign of superabundant grace: the "good wine" that refers to the mystery of Christ's Blood. This leads us directly to Calvary, where Mary stands beneath the Cross together with the other women and with the Apostle John. The Mother and the disciple receive spiritually the testament of Jesus: his last words and his last breath, in which he begins to pour out the Spirit; and they receive the silent cry of his Blood, poured out entirely for us (cf. Jn 19:25-34). Mary knew where that Blood came from: it had been formed within her by the power of the Holy Spirit and she knew that this same creative 'power' was to raise Jesus, as he had promised.

Thus Mary's faith sustained that of the disciples until their encounter with the Risen Lord and continued to accompany them also after his Ascension into Heaven, as they waited for

"[Baptism] in the Holy Spirit" (cf. Acts 1:5). At Pentecost the Virgin Mother appears anew as the Bride of the Spirit, for a universal motherhood of all those who are generated by God through faith in Christ. This is why, for all the generations, Mary is an image and model of the Church which together with the Spirit journeys through time, invoking Jesus' glorious return: "Come, Lord Jesus" (cf. Rv 22:17, 20).

Dear friends, let us too learn at the school of Mary to recognize the presence of the Holy Spirit in our lives, to listen to his inspirations and to follow them with docility. He makes us grow in accordance with the fullness of Christ, in accordance with those good fruits which the Apostle Paul lists in his Letter to the Galatians: "Love, joy, peace, patience, kindness, goodness, faithfulness, gentleness, self-control" (Gal 5:22). I hope you will be filled with these gifts and that you will always walk with Mary, in accordance with the Spirit.

VIII

MARY, WOMAN OF THE EUCHARIST

From the Apostolic Exhortation
Sacramentum Caritatis

THE EUCHARIST AND THE VIRGIN MARY

22 February 2007

33. From the relationship between the Eucharist and the individual sacraments, and from the eschatological significance of the sacred mysteries, the overall shape of the Christian life emerges, a life called at all times to be an act of spiritual worship, a self-offering pleasing to God. Although we are all still journeying towards the complete fulfilment of our hope, this does not mean that we cannot already gratefully acknowledge that God's gifts to us have found their perfect fulfilment in the Virgin Mary, Mother of God and our Mother. Mary's Assumption body and soul into heaven is for us a sign of sure hope, for it shows us, on our pilgrimage through time, the eschatological goal of which the sacrament of the Eucharist enables us even now to have a foretaste.

In Mary most holy, we also see perfectly fulfilled the 'sacramental' way that God comes down to meet his creatures and involves them in his saving work. From the Annunciation to Pentecost, Mary of Nazareth appears as someone whose freedom is completely open to God's will. Her Immaculate Conception is revealed precisely in her unconditional docility to God's word. Obedient faith in response to God's work shapes her life at every moment. A virgin attentive to God's word, she lives in complete harmony with his will; she treasures in her heart the words that come to her from God and, piecing them together like a mosaic, she learns to understand them more deeply (cf. Lk 2:19, 51); Mary is the great Believer who places herself confidently in God's hands, abandoning herself to his will. (102) This mystery deepens as she becomes completely involved in the redemptive mission of Jesus. In the words of the Second Vatican Council, "the blessed Virgin advanced in her pilgrimage of faith, and faithfully persevered in her union with her Son until she stood at the Cross, in keeping with the divine plan (cf. Jn 19:25), suffering deeply with her only-begotten Son, associating herself with his sacrifice in her mother's heart, and lovingly consenting to the immolation of the victim who was born of her. Finally, she was given by the same Christ Jesus, dying on the Cross, as a mother to his disciple, with these words: 'Woman, behold your Son".' (103) From the Annunciation to the Cross, Mary is the one who received the Word, made flesh within her and then silenced in death. It is she, lastly, who took into her arms the lifeless body of the one who truly loved his own "to the end" (Jn 13:1).

Consequently, every time we approach the Body and Blood of Christ in the eucharistic liturgy, we also turn to her who, by her complete fidelity, received Christ's sacrifice for the whole Church. The Synod Fathers rightly declared that "Mary inaugurates the Church's participation in the sacrifice of the Redeemer." (104) She is the Immaculata, who receives God's gift unconditionally and is thus associated with his work of salvation. Mary of Nazareth, icon of the nascent Church, is the model for each of us, called to receive the gift that Jesus makes of himself in the Eucharist.

96. May Mary Most Holy, the Immaculate Virgin, ark of the new and eternal covenant, accompany us on our way to meet the Lord who comes. In her we find realized most perfectly the essence of the Church. The Church sees in Mary – "Woman of

the Eucharist", as she was called by the Servant of God John Paul II (253) – her finest icon, and she contemplates Mary as a singular model of the eucharistic life. For this reason, as the priest prepares to receive on the altar the *verum Corpus natum de Maria Virgine*, speaking on behalf of the liturgical assembly, he says in the words of the canon: "We honour Mary, the ever-virgin mother of Jesus Christ our Lord and God" (254). Her holy name is also invoked and venerated in the canons of the Eastern Christian traditions. The faithful, for their part, "commend to Mary, Mother of the Church, their lives and the work of their hands. Striving to have the same sentiments as Mary, they help the whole community to become a living offering pleasing to the Father" (255). She is the *tota pulchra*, the all-beautiful, for in her the radiance of God's glory shines forth. The beauty of the heavenly liturgy, which must be reflected in our own assemblies, is faithfully mirrored in her. From Mary we must learn to become men and women of the Eucharist and of the Church, and thus to present ourselves, in the words of Saint Paul, "holy and blameless" before the Lord, even as he wished us to be from the beginning (cf. Col 1:22; Eph 1:4) (256).

97. Through the intercession of the Blessed Virgin Mary, may the Holy Spirit kindle within us the same ardour experienced by the disciples on the way to Emmaus (cf. Lk 24:13-35) and renew our 'eucharistic wonder' through the splendour and beauty radiating from the liturgical rite, the efficacious sign of the infinite beauty of the holy mystery of God. Those disciples arose and returned in haste to Jerusalem in order to share their joy with their brothers and sisters in the faith. True joy is found in recognizing that the Lord is still with us, our faithful companion along the way. The Eucharist makes us discover that Christ, risen from the dead, is our contemporary in the mystery of the Church, his body. Of this mystery of love we have become witnesses. Let us encourage one another to walk joyfully, our

hearts filled with wonder, towards our encounter with the Holy Eucharist, so that we may experience and proclaim to others the truth of the words with which Jesus took leave of his disciples: "Lo, I am with you always, until the end of the world" (Mt 28:20).

(102) Cf. Benedict XVI, Homily (8 December 2005): AAS 98 (2006), 15-16.
(103) Dogmatic Constitution on the Church *Lumen Gentium*, n.58.
(104) *Propositio* 4.

(253) Cf. John Paul II, Encyclical Letter *Ecclesia de Eucharistia* (17 April 2003), 53: AAS 95 (2003), 469.
(254) Eucharistic Prayer I (Roman Canon).
(255) *Propositio* 50.
(256) Cf. Benedict XVI, Homily (8 December 2005): AAS 98 (2006), 15.

From the

ANGELUS

St Peter's Square
Sunday, 14 June 2009

We can imagine with what great faith and love Our Lady must have received and adored the Blessed Eucharist in her heart! For her it must have been every time like reliving the whole mystery of her Son Jesus: from his Conception to his Resurrection. The "Woman of the Eucharist", my venerable and beloved Predecessor John Paul II called her. Let us learn from her to renew our Communion with the Body of Christ ceaselessly so that we may love one another as he loved us.

IX
ASSUMPTION

From the Homily given at

MASS ON THE SOLEMNITY OF THE ASSUMPTION OF THE BLESSED VIRGIN MARY

Parish Church of Castel Gandolfo
Monday, 15 August 2005

The Feast of the Assumption is a day of joy. God has won. Love has won. It has won life. Love has shown that it is stronger than death, that God possesses the true strength and that his strength is goodness and love.

Mary was taken up body and soul into Heaven: there is even room in God for the body. Heaven is no longer a very remote sphere unknown to us.

We have a Mother in Heaven. And the Mother of God, the Mother of the Son of God, is our Mother. He himself has said so. He made her our Mother when he said to the disciple and to all of us: "Behold, your Mother!" We have a Mother in Heaven. Heaven is open, Heaven has a heart.

In the Gospel we heard the *Magnificat,* that great poem inspired by the Holy Spirit that came from Mary's lips, indeed, from Mary's heart. This marvellous canticle mirrors the entire soul, the entire personality of Mary. We can say that this hymn of hers is a portrait of Mary, a true icon in which we can see her exactly as she is. I would like to highlight only two points in this great canticle.

It begins with the word 'Magnificat': my soul 'magnifies' the Lord, that is, 'proclaims the greatness' of the Lord. Mary wanted

God to be great in the world, great in her life and present among us all. She was not afraid that God might be a 'rival' in our life, that with his greatness he might encroach on our freedom, our vital space. She knew that if God is great, we too are great. Our life is not oppressed but raised and expanded: it is precisely then that it becomes great in the splendour of God.

The fact that our first parents thought the contrary was the core of original sin. They feared that if God were too great, he would take something away from their life. They thought that they could set God aside to make room for themselves.

This was also the great temptation of the modern age, of the past three or four centuries. More and more people have thought and said: "But this God does not give us our freedom; with all his commandments, he restricts the space in our lives. So God has to disappear; we want to be autonomous and independent. Without this God we ourselves would be gods and do as we pleased."

This was also the view of the Prodigal Son, who did not realize that he was 'free' precisely because he was in his father's house. He left for distant lands and squandered his estate. In the end, he realized that precisely because he had gone so far away from his father, instead of being free he had become a slave; he understood that only by returning home to his father's house would he be truly free, in the full beauty of life.

This is how it is in our modern epoch. Previously, it was thought and believed that by setting God aside and being autonomous, following only our own ideas and inclinations, we would truly be free to do whatever we liked without anyone being able to give us orders. But when God disappears, men and women do not become greater; indeed, they lose the divine dignity, their faces lose God's splendour. In the end, they turn out to be merely products of a blind evolution and, as such, can be used and abused. This is precisely what the experience of our epoch has confirmed for us.

Only if God is great is humankind also great. With Mary, we must begin to understand that this is so. We must not drift away from God but make God present; we must ensure that he is great in our lives. Thus, we too will become divine; all the splendour of the divine dignity will then be ours. Let us apply this to our own lives.

It is important that God be great among us, in public and in private life.

In public life, it is important that God be present, for example, through the cross on public buildings, and that he be present in our community life, for only if God is present do we have an orientation, a common direction; otherwise, disputes become impossible to settle, for our common dignity is no longer recognized.

Let us make God great in public and in private life. This means making room for God in our lives every day, starting in the morning with prayers, and then dedicating time to God, giving Sundays to God. We do not waste our free time if we offer it to God. If God enters into our time, all time becomes greater, roomier, richer.

A second observation: Mary's poem – the *Magnificat* – is quite original; yet at the same time, it is a 'fabric' woven throughout of 'threads' from the Old Testament, of words of God.

Thus, we see that Mary was, so to speak, 'at home' with God's word, she lived on God's word, she was penetrated by God's word. To the extent that she spoke with God's words, she thought with God's words, her thoughts were God's thoughts, her words, God's words. She was penetrated by divine light and this is why she was so resplendent, so good, so radiant with love and goodness.

Mary lived on the Word of God, she was imbued with the Word of God. And the fact that she was immersed in the Word of God and was totally familiar with the Word also endowed her later with the inner enlightenment of wisdom.

Whoever thinks with God thinks well, and whoever speaks to God speaks well. They have valid criteria to judge all the things of the world. They become prudent, wise, and at the same time good; they also become strong and courageous with the strength of God, who resists evil and fosters good in the world.

Thus, Mary speaks with us, speaks to us, invites us to know the Word of God, to love the Word of God, to live with the Word of God, to think with the Word of God. And we can do so in many different ways: by reading Sacred Scripture, by participating especially in the Liturgy, in which Holy Church throughout the year opens the entire book of Sacred Scripture to us. She opens it to our lives and makes it present in our lives.

But I am also thinking of the *Compendium* of the *Catechism of the Catholic Church* that we recently published, in which the Word of God is applied to our lives and the reality of our lives interpreted; it helps us enter into the great 'temple' of God's Word, to learn to love it and, like Mary, to be penetrated by this Word.

Thus, life becomes luminous and we have the basic criterion with which to judge; at the same time, we receive goodness and strength.

Mary is taken up body and soul into the glory of Heaven, and with God and in God she is Queen of Heaven and earth. And is she really so remote from us?

The contrary is true. Precisely because she is with God and in God, she is very close to each one of us.

While she lived on this earth she could only be close to a few people. Being in God, who is close to us, actually, 'within' all of us, Mary shares in this closeness of God. Being in God and with God, she is close to each one of us, knows our hearts, can hear our prayers, can help us with her motherly kindness and has been given to us, as the Lord said, precisely as a "mother" to whom we can turn at every moment.

She always listens to us, she is always close to us, and being Mother of the Son, participates in the power of the Son and in his goodness. We can always entrust the whole of our lives to this Mother, who is not far from any one of us.

On this feast day, let us thank the Lord for the gift of the Mother, and let us pray to Mary to help us find the right path every day. Amen.

Homily given at

MASS ON THE SOLEMNITY OF THE ASSUMPTION OF THE BLESSED VIRGIN MARY

Parish Church of St Thomas of Villanova,
Castel Gandolfo
Tuesday, 15 August 2006

In the *Magnificat*, the great hymn of Our Lady that we have just heard in the Gospel, we find some surprising words. Mary says: "Henceforth all generations will call me blessed". The Mother of the Lord prophesies the Marian praises of the Church for all of the future, the Marian devotion of the People of God until the end of time. In praising Mary, the Church did not invent something 'adjacent' to Scripture: she responded to this prophecy which Mary made at that moment of grace.

And Mary's words were not only personal, perhaps arbitrary words. Elizabeth, filled with the Holy Spirit as St Luke said, exclaimed with a loud cry: "Blessed is she who believed . . .". And Mary, also filled with the Holy Spirit, continues and completes what Elizabeth said, affirming: "all generations will call me blessed". It is a real prophesy, inspired by the Holy Spirit, and in venerating Mary, the Church responds to a command of the Holy Spirit; she does what she has to do.

We do not praise God sufficiently by keeping silent about his saints, especially Mary, "the Holy One" who became his dwelling place on earth. The simple and multiform light of God appears to us exactly in its variety and richness only in the countenance of the saints, who are the true mirrors of his light. And it is precisely by looking at Mary's face that we can see more clearly than in any other way the beauty, goodness and mercy of God. In her face we can truly perceive the divine light.

"All generations will call me blessed". We can praise Mary, we can venerate Mary for she is "blessed", she is blessed for ever. And this is the subject of this Feast. She is blessed because she is united to God, she lives with God and in God.

On the eve of his Passion, taking leave of his disciples, the Lord said: "In my Father's house are many rooms . . . I go to prepare a place for you."

By saying, "I am the handmaid of the Lord; let it be done to me according to your word", Mary prepared God's dwelling here on earth; with her body and soul, she became his dwelling place and thereby opened the earth to heaven.

In the Gospel we have just heard, St Luke, with various allusions, makes us understand that Mary is the true Ark of the Covenant, that the mystery of the Temple – God's dwelling place here on earth – is fulfilled in Mary. God, who became present here on earth, truly dwells in Mary. Mary becomes his tent. What all the cultures desire – that God dwell among us – is brought about here.

St Augustine says: "Before conceiving the Lord in her body she had already conceived him in her soul." She had made room for the Lord in her soul and thus really became the true Temple where God made himself incarnate, where he became present on this earth.

Thus, being God's dwelling place on earth, in her the eternal dwelling place has already been prepared, it has already been prepared for ever. And this constitutes the whole content of the Dogma of the Assumption of Mary, body and soul, into heavenly glory, expressed here in these words. Mary is "blessed" because – totally, in body and soul and for ever – she became the

Lord's dwelling place. If this is true, Mary does not merely invite our admiration and veneration, but she guides us, shows us the way of life, shows us how we can become blessed, how to find the path of happiness.

Let us listen once again to Elizabeth's words fulfilled in Mary's *Magnificat*: "Blessed is she who believed". The first and fundamental act in order to become a dwelling place of God and thus find definitive happiness is to believe: it is faith, faith in God, in that God who showed himself in Jesus Christ and makes himself heard in the divine Word of Holy Scripture.

Believing is not adding one opinion to others. And the conviction, the belief, that God exists is not information like any other. Regarding most information, it makes no difference to us whether it is true or false; it does not change our lives. But if God does not exist, life is empty, the future is empty. And if God exists, everything changes, life is light, our future is light and we have guidance for how to live. Therefore, believing constitutes the fundamental orientation of our life. To believe, to say: "Yes, I believe that you are God, I believe that you are present among us in the Incarnate Son", gives my life a direction, impels me to be attached to God, to unite with God and so to find my dwelling place, and the way to live.

To believe is not only a way of thinking or an idea; as has already been mentioned, it is a way of acting, a manner of living. To believe means to follow the trail indicated to us by the Word of God. In addition to this fundamental act of faith, which is an existential act, a position taken for the whole of life, Mary adds another word: "His mercy is on those who fear him".

Together with the whole of Scripture, she is speaking of "fear of God". Perhaps this is a phrase with which we are not very familiar or do not like very much. But "fear of God" is not anguish; it is something quite different. As children, we are not anxious about the Father but we have fear of God, the concern not to destroy the love on which our life is based.

Fear of God is that sense of responsibility that we are bound to possess, responsibility for the portion of the world that has been entrusted to us in our lives. It is responsibility for the good administration of this portion of the world and of history, and one thus helps the just building of the world, contributing to the victory of goodness and peace.

"All generations will call you blessed": this means that the future, what is to come, belongs to God, it is in God's hands, that it is God who conquers.

Nor does he conquer the mighty dragon of which today's First Reading speaks, the dragon that represents all the powers of violence in the world. They seem invincible but Mary tells us that they are not invincible.

The Woman – as the First Reading and the Gospel show us – is stronger, because God is stronger. Of course, in comparison with the dragon, so heavily armed, this Woman who is Mary, who is the Church, seems vulnerable or defenceless. And truly God is vulnerable in the world, because he is Love and love is vulnerable. Yet he holds the future in his hands: it is love, not hatred, that triumphs; it is peace that is victorious in the end.

This is the great consolation contained in the Dogma of Mary's Assumption body and soul into heavenly glory. Let us thank the Lord for this consolation but let us also see it as a commitment for us to take the side of good and peace. And let us pray to Mary, Queen of Peace, to help peace to be victorious today: "Queen of Peace, pray for us!" Amen!

GENERAL AUDIENCE

Castel Gandolfo
Wednesday, 16 August 2006

Meditation on the Solemnity of the Assumption of the Blessed Virgin Mary

Today, our customary weekly Wednesday appointment is again taking place in the atmosphere of the Solemnity of the Blessed Virgin Mary's Assumption. I would therefore like to ask you to turn your gaze once again to our heavenly Mother, whom yesterday's liturgy helped us to contemplate triumphant with Christ in Heaven.

Since the first centuries of Christianity, the Christian people has always found this feast deeply stirring; as is well known, it celebrates the glorification, also in body, of that creature whom God chose as Mother and whom Jesus on the Cross gave as Mother to the whole of humanity.

The Assumption evokes a mystery that concerns each one of us because, as the Second Vatican Council affirms, Mary "shines forth on earth . . . a sign of certain hope and comfort to the pilgrim People of God" (*Lumen Gentium*, n. 68).

However, taken up by the events of each day, one can sometimes forget this comforting spiritual reality that constitutes an important truth of faith; so how can it be ensured that this luminous sign of hope is ever more clearly perceived by all of us and by contemporary society?

Some people today live as if they never had to die or as if, with death, everything were over; others, who hold that man is the one and only author of his own destiny, behave as though God did not exist, and at times they even reach the point of denying that there is room for him in our world.

Yet, the great breakthroughs of technology and science that have considerably improved humanity's condition leave unresolved the deepest searchings of the human soul.

Only openness to the mystery of God, who is Love, can quench the thirst for truth and happiness in our hearts; only the prospect of eternity can give authentic value to historical events and especially to the mystery of human frailty, suffering and death.

By contemplating Mary in heavenly glory, we understand that the earth is not the definitive homeland for us either, and that if we live with our gaze fixed on eternal goods we will one day share in this same glory and the earth will become more beautiful.

Consequently, we must not lose our serenity and peace even amid the thousands of daily difficulties. The luminous sign of Our Lady taken up into Heaven shines out even more brightly when sad shadows of suffering and violence seem to loom on the horizon.

We may be sure of it: from on high, Mary follows our footsteps with gentle concern, dispels the gloom in moments of darkness and distress, reassures us with her motherly hand.

Supported by awareness of this, let us continue confidently on our path of Christian commitment wherever Providence may lead us. Let us forge ahead in our lives under Mary's guidance.

Homily given during

HOLY MASS ON THE SOLEMNITY OF THE ASSUMPTION OF THE BLESSED VIRGIN MARY

St Thomas of Villanova Parish, Castel Gandolfo
Wednesday, 15 August 2007

In his great work *De Civitate Dei*, St Augustine says once that the whole of human history, the history of the world, is a struggle between two loves: love of God to the point of losing oneself, of total self-giving, and love of oneself to the point of despising God, of hating others. This same interpretation of history as a struggle between two loves, between love and selfishness, also appears in the reading from the Book of Revelation that we have just heard.

Here, these two loves appear in two great figures. First of all, there is the immensely strong, red dragon with a striking and disturbing manifestation of power without grace, without love, of absolute selfishness, terror and violence.

At the time when St John wrote the Book of Revelation, this dragon represented for him the power of the anti-Christian Roman Emperors, from Nero to Domitian. This power seemed boundless; the military, political and propagandist power of the Roman Empire was such that before it, faith, the Church, appeared as a defenceless woman with no chance of survival and even less of victory.

Who could stand up to this omnipresent force that seemed capable of achieving everything? Yet, we know that in the end it was the defenceless woman who won and not egoism or hatred; the love of God triumphed and the Roman Empire was opened to the Christian faith.

The words of Sacred Scripture always transcend the period in history. Thus, not only does this dragon suggest the anti-Christian power of the persecutors of the Church of that time, but also anti-Christian dictatorships of all periods.

We see this power, the force of the red dragon, brought into existence once again in the great dictatorships of the last century: the Nazi dictatorship and the dictatorship of Stalin monopolized all the power, penetrated every corner, the very last corner. It seemed impossible in the long term that faith could survive in the face of this dragon that was so powerful, that could not wait to devour God become a Child, as well as the woman, the Church. But also in this case, in the end love was stronger than hate.

Today too, the dragon exists in new and different ways. It exists in the form of materialistic ideologies that tell us it is absurd to think of God; it is absurd to observe God's commandments: they are a leftover from a time past. Life is only worth living for its own sake. Take everything we can get in this brief moment of life. Consumerism, selfishness and entertainment alone are worthwhile. This is life. This is how we must live. And once again, it seems absurd, impossible, to oppose this dominant mindset with all its media and propagandist power. Today too, it seems impossible to imagine a God who created man and made himself a Child and who was to be the true ruler of the world.

Even now, this dragon appears invincible, but it is still true today that God is stronger than the dragon, that it is love which conquers rather than selfishness.

Having thus considered the various historical forms of the

dragon, let us now look at the other image: the woman clothed with the sun, with the moon under her feet, surrounded by 12 stars. This is also a multidimensional image.

Without any doubt, a first meaning is that it is Our Lady, Mary, clothed with the sun, that is, with God, totally; Mary who lives totally in God, surrounded and penetrated by God's light. Surrounded by the 12 stars, that is, by the 12 tribes of Israel, by the whole People of God, by the whole Communion of Saints; and at her feet, the moon, the image of death and mortality.

Mary has left death behind her; she is totally clothed in life, she is taken up body and soul into God's glory and thus, placed in glory after overcoming death, she says to us: Take heart, it is love that wins in the end! The message of my life was: I am the handmaid of God, my life has been a gift of myself to God and my neighbour. And this life of service now arrives in real life. May you too have trust and have the courage to live like this, countering all the threats of the dragon.

This is the first meaning of the woman whom Mary succeeded in being. The "woman clothed with the sun" is the great sign of the victory of love, of the victory of goodness, of the victory of God; a great sign of consolation.

Yet, this woman who suffered, who had to flee, who gave birth with cries of anguish, is also the Church, the pilgrim Church of all times. In all generations she has to give birth to Christ anew, to bring him very painfully into the world, with great suffering. Persecuted in all ages, it is almost as if, pursued by the dragon, she had gone to live in the wilderness.

However, in all ages, the Church, the People of God, also lives by the light of God and as the Gospel says is nourished by God, nourishing herself with the Bread of the Holy Eucharist. Thus, in all the trials in the various situations of the Church through the ages in different parts of the world, she wins through suffering. And she is the presence, the guarantee of God's love against all the ideologies of hatred and selfishness.

We see of course that today too the dragon wants to devour God who made himself a Child. Do not fear for this seemingly frail God; the fight has already been won. Today too, this weak God is strong: he is true strength.

Thus, the Feast of the Assumption is an invitation to trust in God and also to imitate Mary in what she herself said: Behold, I am the handmaid of the Lord; I put myself at the Lord's disposal.

This is the lesson: one should travel one's own path; one should give life and not take it. And precisely in this way each one is on the journey of love which is the loss of self, but this losing of oneself is in fact the only way to truly find oneself, to find true life.

Let us look to Mary, taken up into Heaven. Let us be encouraged to celebrate the joyful feast with faith: God wins. Faith, which seems weak, is the true force of the world. Love is stronger than hate. And let us say with Elizabeth: Blessed are you among women. Let us pray to you with all the Church: Holy Mary, Mother of God, pray for us sinners, now and at the hour of our death. Amen.

Homily given on the

SOLEMNITY OF THE ASSUMPTION OF THE BLESSED VIRGIN MARY

St Thomas of Villanova Parish, Castel Gandolfo
Friday, 15 August 2008

The Solemnity of the Assumption of the Blessed Virgin Mary, the oldest Marian Feast, returns every year in the heart of summer. It is an opportunity to rise with Mary to the heights of the spirit where one breathes the pure air of supernatural life and contemplates the most authentic beauty, the beauty of holiness. The atmosphere of today's celebration is steeped in paschal joy. "Today", the antiphon of the *Magnificat* says, "the Virgin Mary was taken up to Heaven. Rejoice, for she reigns with Christ for ever. Alleluia." This proclamation speaks to us of an event that is utterly unique and extraordinary, yet destined to fill the heart of every human being with hope and happiness. Mary is indeed the first fruit of the new humanity, the creature in whom the mystery of Christ – his Incarnation, death, Resurrection and Ascension into Heaven – has already fully taken effect, redeeming her from death and conveying her, body and soul, to the Kingdom of immortal life. For this reason, as the Second Vatican Council recalls, the Virgin Mary is a sign of certain hope and comfort to us (cf. *Lumen Gentium,* n. 68). Today's feast impels us to lift our gaze to Heaven; not to a heaven consisting of abstract ideas or even an imaginary heaven created by art, but the Heaven of true reality which is God himself. God is Heaven. He is our destination, the destination and the eternal dwelling place from which we come and for which we are striving.

St Germanus, Bishop of Constantinople in the eighth century, in a homily given on the Feast of the Assumption, addressing the heavenly Mother of God said: "You are the One who through your immaculate flesh reunited the Christian people with Christ. . . . Just as all who thirst hasten to the fountain, so every soul hastens to you, the Fountain of love, and as every man aspires to live, to see the light that never fades, so every Christian longs to enter the light of the Most Blessed Trinity where you already are." It is these same sentiments that inspire us today as we contemplate Mary in God's glory. In fact, when she fell asleep in this world to reawaken in Heaven, she simply followed her Son Jesus for the last time, on his longest and most crucial journey, his passage "from this world to the Father" (cf. Jn 13: 1).

Like him, together with him, she departed this world to return "to the Father's House" (cf. Jn 14: 2). And all this is not remote from us as it might seem at first sight, because we are all children of the Father, God; we are all brothers and sisters of Jesus and we are all also children of Mary, our Mother. And we all aspire to happiness. And the happiness to which we all aspire is God, so we are all journeying on toward this happiness we call Heaven which in reality is God. And Mary helps us, she encourages us to ensure that every moment of our life is a step forward on this exodus, on this journey toward God. May she help us in this way to make the reality of heaven, God's greatness, also present in the life of our world. Is this not basically the paschal dynamism of the human being, of every person who wants to become heavenly, perfectly happy, by virtue of Christ's Resurrection? And might this not be the beginning and anticipation of a movement that involves every human being and the entire cosmos? She, from whom God took his flesh and whose soul was pierced by a sword on Calvary, was associated first and uniquely in the mystery of this transformation for which we, also often pierced by the sword of suffering in this world, are all striving.

The new Eve followed the new Adam in suffering, in the Passion, and so too in definitive joy. Christ is the first fruits but his risen flesh is inseparable from that of his earthly Mother, Mary. In Mary all humanity is involved in the Assumption to God, and together with her all creation, whose groans and sufferings, St Paul tells us, are the birth-pangs of the new humanity. Thus are born the new Heaven and the new earth in which death shall be no more, neither shall there be mourning nor crying nor pain any more (cf. Rv 21: 1-4).

What a great mystery of love is presented to us once again today for our contemplation! Christ triumphed over death with the omnipotence of his love. Love alone is omnipotent. This love impelled Christ to die for us and thus to overcome death. Yes, love alone gives access to the Kingdom of life! And Mary entered after her Son, associated with his Glory, after being associated with his Passion. She entered it with an uncontainable force, keeping the way behind her open to us all. And for this reason we invoke her today as "Gate of Heaven", "Queen of Angels" and "Refuge of sinners". It is certainly not reasoning that will make us understand this reality which is so sublime, but rather simple, forthright faith and the silence of prayer that puts us in touch with the Mystery that infinitely exceeds us. Prayer helps us speak with God and hear how the Lord speaks to our heart.

Let us ask Mary today to make us the gift of her faith, that faith which enables us already to live in the dimension between finite and infinite, that faith which also transforms the sentiment of time and the passing of our existence, that faith in which we are profoundly aware that our life is not stuck in the past but attracted towards the future, towards God, where Christ, and behind him Mary, has preceded us.

By looking at Mary's Assumption into Heaven we understand

better that even though our daily life may be marked by trials and difficulties, it flows like a river to the divine ocean, to the fullness of joy and peace. We understand that our death is not the end but rather the entrance into life that knows no death. Our setting on the horizon of this world is our rising at the dawn of the new world, the dawn of the eternal day.

"Mary, while you accompany us in the toil of our daily living and dying, keep us constantly oriented to the true homeland of bliss. Help us to do as you did."

Dear brothers and sisters, dear friends who are taking part in this celebration this morning, let us pray this prayer to Mary together. In the face of the sad spectacle of all the false joy and at the same time of all the anguished suffering which is spreading through the world, we must learn from her to become ourselves signs of hope and comfort; we must proclaim with our own lives Christ's Resurrection.

"Help us, Mother, bright Gate of Heaven, Mother of Mercy, source through whom came Jesus Christ, our life and our joy. Amen."

From the

GENERAL AUDIENCE

Papal Summer Residence, Castel Gandolfo
Wednesday, 13 August 2008

Those who pray never lose hope, even when they find themselves in a difficult and even humanly hopeless plight. Sacred Scripture teaches us this and Church history bears witness to this.

In fact, how many examples we could cite of situations in which it was precisely prayer that sustained the journey of Saints and of the Christian people! Among the testimonies of our epoch I would like to mention the examples of two Saints whom we are commemorating in these days: Teresa Benedicta of the Cross, Edith Stein, whose feast we celebrated on 9 August, and Maximilian Mary Kolbe, whom we will commemorate tomorrow, on 14 August, the eve of the Solemnity of the Assumption of the Blessed Virgin Mary. Both ended their earthly life with martyrdom in the concentration camp of Auschwitz. Their lives might seem to have been a defeat, but it is precisely in their martyrdom that the brightness of Love which dispels the gloom of selfishness and hatred shines forth. The following words are attributed to St Maximilian Kolbe, who is said to have spoken them when the Nazi persecution was raging: "Hatred is not a creative force: only love is creative." And heroic proof of his love was the generous offering he made of himself in exchange for a fellow prisoner, an offer that culminated in his death in the starvation bunker on 14 August 1941.

On 6 August the following year, three days before her tragic end, Edith Stein approaching some Sisters in the monastery of Echt, in the Netherlands, said to them: "I am ready for anything. Jesus is also here in our midst. Thus far I have been able to pray very well and I have said with all my heart: *Ave, Crux, spes unica.*" Witnesses who managed to escape the terrible massacre recounted that while Teresa Benedicta of the Cross, dressed in the Carmelite habit, was making her way, consciously, toward death, she distinguished herself by her conduct full of peace, her serene attitude and her calm behaviour, attentive to the needs of all. Prayer was the secret of this Saint, Co-Patroness of Europe, who, *"Even after she found the truth in the peace of the contemplative life, she was to live to the full the mystery of the Cross"* (Apostolic Letter *Spes Aedificandi*).

"Hail Mary!" was the last prayer on the lips of St Maximilian Mary Kolbe, as he offered his arm to the person who was about to kill him with an injection of carbolic acid. It is moving to note how humble and trusting recourse to Our Lady is always a source of courage and serenity. While we prepare to celebrate the Solemnity of the Assumption, which is one of the best-loved Marian feasts in the Christian tradition, let us renew our entrustment to her who from Heaven watches over us with motherly love at every moment. In fact, we say this in the familiar prayer of the Hail Mary, asking her to pray for us "now and at the hour of our death."

Homily from the

HOLY MASS ON THE SOLEMNITY OF THE ASSUMPTION OF THE BLESSED VIRGIN MARY

St Thomas of Villanova Parish, Castel Gandolfo
Saturday, 15 August 2009

Today's Solemnity crowns the series of important liturgical celebrations in which we are called to contemplate the role of the Blessed Virgin Mary in the history of salvation. Indeed, the Immaculate Conception, the Annunciation, the Divine Motherhood and the Assumption are the fundamental, interconnected milestones with which the Church exalts and praises the glorious destiny of the Mother of God, but in which we can also read our history. The mystery of Mary's conception recalls the first page of the human event, pointing out to us that in the divine plan of creation man was to have had the purity and beauty of the Virgin Immaculate. This plan, jeopardized but not destroyed by sin, through the Incarnation of the Son of God, proclaimed and brought into being in Mary, was recomposed and restored to the free acceptance of the human being in faith. Lastly, in Mary's Assumption, we contemplate what we ourselves are called to attain in the following of Christ the Lord and in obedience to his word, at the end of our earthly journey.

The last stage of the Mother of God's earthly pilgrimage invites us to look at the manner in which she journeyed on toward the goal of glorious eternity.

In the Gospel passage just proclaimed, St Luke tells that, after the Angel's announcement, Mary "arose and went with haste into the hill country", to visit Elizabeth (Lk 1: 39). With these words the Evangelist wishes to emphasize that for Mary to follow her own vocation in docility to God's Spirit, who has brought about within her the Incarnation of the Word, means taking a new road and immediately setting out from home, allowing herself to be led on a journey by God alone. St Ambrose, commenting on Mary's "haste", says: "the grace of the Holy Spirit admits of no delay" (*Expos. Evang. sec. Lucam,* II, 19: *PL* 15, 1560). Our Lady's life is guided by Another: "Behold, I am the handmaid of the Lord; let it be to me according to your word" (Lk 1: 38); it is modelled by the Holy Spirit, it is marked by events and encounters, such as that with Elizabeth, but above all by her very special relationship with her Son Jesus. It is a journey on which Mary, cherishing and pondering in her heart the events of her own life, perceives in them ever more profoundly the mysterious design of God the Father for the salvation of the world.

Then, by following Jesus from Bethlehem to exile in Egypt, in both his hidden and his public life and even to the foot of the Cross, Mary lives her constant ascent to God in the spirit of the *Magnificat,* fully adhering to God's plan of love, even in moments of darkness and suffering, and nourishing in her heart total abandonment in the Lord's hands in order to be a paradigm for the faithful of the Church (cf. *Lumen Gentium*, nn. 64-65).

The whole of life is an ascent, the whole of life is meditation, obedience, trust and hope, even in darkness; and the whole of life is marked by this "holy haste" which knows that God always has priority and nothing else must create haste in our existence.

And, lastly, the Assumption reminds us that Mary's life, like that of every Christian, is a journey of following, following Jesus, a journey that has a very precise destination, a future already marked out: the definitive victory over sin and death and full communion with God, because as Paul says in his Letter to the Ephesians the Father "raised us up with him, and made us sit with him in the heavenly places in Christ Jesus" (Eph 2: 6). This means that with Baptism we have already fundamentally been raised and are seated in the heavenly places in Christ Jesus, but we must physically attain what was previously begun and brought about in Baptism. In us, union with Christ, the resurrection, is incomplete; but for the Virgin Mary it is complete, despite the journey that Our Lady also had to make. She has entered into the fullness of union with God, with her Son, and she draws us onwards and accompanies us on our journey.

In Mary taken up into Heaven we therefore contemplate the One who, through a unique privilege, was granted to share with her soul and her body in Christ's definitive victory over death. "When her earthly life was over", the Second Vatican Council says, the Immaculate Virgin "was taken up body and soul into heavenly glory . . . and exalted by the Lord as Queen over all things, that she might be the more fully conformed to her Son, the Lord of lords (cf. Rv 19: 16) and conqueror of sin and death" (*Lumen Gentium,* n. 59). In the Virgin taken up into Heaven we contemplate the crowning of her faith, of that journey of faith which she points out to the Church and to each one of us: the One who, at every moment, welcomed the Word of God, is taken up into Heaven, in other words she herself is received by the Son in the "dwelling place" which he prepared for us with his death and Resurrection (cf. Jn 14: 2-3).

Human life on earth as the First Reading has reminded us is a journey that takes place, constantly, in the intense struggle between the dragon and the woman, between good and evil. This is the plight of human history: it is like a voyage on a sea, often dark and stormy. Mary is the Star that guides us towards her Son Jesus, "the sun that has risen above all the shadows of history" (cf. *Spe Salvi,* n. 49) and gives us the hope we need: the hope that we can win, that God has won and that, with Baptism, we entered into this victory. We do not succumb definitively: God helps us, he guides us.

This is our hope: this presence of the Lord within us that becomes visible in Mary taken up into Heaven. 'The Virgin', in a little while we shall read in the Preface for this Solemnity that you made to shine out as "a sign of hope and comfort for your people on their pilgrim way."

With St Bernard, a mystic who sang the Blessed Virgin's praises, let us thus invoke her: "We pray you, O Blessed One, for the grace that you found, for those prerogatives that you deserved, for the Mercy you bore, obtain that the One who for your sake deigned to share in our wretchedness and infirmity, through your prayers may make us share in his graces, in his bliss and in his eternal glory, Jesus Christ, your Son, our Lord, who is above all things, Blessed God for ever and ever. Amen" (*Sermo* 2 "de Adventu", 5: *PL* 183, 43).

ANGELUS

Courtyard of Castel Gandolfo
Saturday, 15 August 2009

In the heart of the month of August, a holiday period for many families and also for me, the Church celebrates the Solemnity of the Assumption of the Blessed Virgin. This is a privileged opportunity to meditate on the ultimate meaning of our existence, helped by today's Liturgy which invites us to live in this world oriented to eternal happiness in order to share in the same glory as Mary, the same joy as our Mother (cf. Opening Prayer). Let us, therefore, turn our gaze to Our Lady, Star of Hope, who illumines us on our earthly journey, and follow the example of the Saints who turned to her in every circumstance. You know that we are celebrating the Year for Priests in remembrance of the Holy Curé d'Ars, and I would like to draw from the thoughts and testimonies of this holy country parish priest some ideas for reflection that will be able to help all of us especially us priests to strengthen our love and veneration for the Most Holy Virgin.

His biographers claim that St John Mary Vianney spoke to Our Lady with devotion and, at the same time, with trust and spontaneity. "The Blessed Virgin", he used to say, "is immaculate and adorned with all the virtues that make her so beautiful and pleasing to the Blessed Trinity." And further: "The heart of this good Mother is nothing but love and mercy, all she wants is to see us happy. To be heard, it suffices to address oneself to her." The priest's zeal shines through these words. Motivated by apostolic longing, he rejoiced in speaking to his faithful of Mary and never tired of doing so. He could even present a difficult mystery like today's, that of the Assumption, with effective images, such as, for example: "Man was created for Heaven. The devil broke the ladder that led to it. Our Lord, with his Passion, made another. . . . The Virgin Most Holy stands at the top of the ladder and holds it steady with both hands."

The Holy Curé d'Ars was attracted above all by Mary's beauty, a beauty that coincides with her being Immaculate, the only creature to have been conceived without a shadow of sin. "The Blessed Virgin", he said, "is that beautiful Creature who never displeased the good Lord." As a good and faithful pastor, he first of all set an example also in this filial love for the Mother of Jesus by whom he felt drawn toward Heaven. "Were I not to go to Heaven", he exclaimed, "how sorry I should be! I should never see the Blessed Virgin, this most beautiful creature!" Moreover, on several occasions he consecrated his parish to Our Lady, recommending that mothers in particular do the same, every morning, with their children. Dear brothers and sisters, let us make our own the sentiments of the Holy Curé d'Ars. And with his same faith let us turn to Mary, taken up into Heaven, in a special way entrusting to her the priests of the whole world.

ANGELUS

Courtyard of Castel Gandolfo
Sunday, 16 August 2009

Yesterday we celebrated the great Feast of Mary taken up into Heaven, and today we read these words of Jesus in the Gospel: "I am the living bread which came down from heaven" (Jn 6: 51).

One cannot but be struck by this parallel that rotates around the symbol of "Heaven": Mary was "taken up" to the very place from which her Son had "come down". Of course, this language, which is biblical, expresses in figurative terms something that never completely coincides with the world of our own concepts and images. But let us pause for a moment to think! Jesus presents himself as the "living bread", that is, the food which contains the life of God itself which it can communicate to those who eat it, the true nourishment that gives life, which is really and deeply nourishing. Jesus says: "if any one eats of this bread, he will live for ever; and the bread which I shall give for the life of the world is my flesh" (Jn 6: 51). Well, *from whom* did the Son of God take his "flesh", his actual, earthly humanity? He took it from the Virgin Mary. In order to enter our mortal condition, God took from her a human body. In turn, at the end of her earthly life, the Virgin's body was taken up into Heaven by God and brought to enter the heavenly condition. It is a sort of exchange in which God always takes the full initiative but, in a certain sense, as we have seen on other occasions, he also needs Mary, her 'yes' as a creature, her very flesh, her actual existence, in order to prepare the matter for his sacrifice: the Body and the Blood, to offer them on the Cross as a means of eternal life and, in the sacrament of the Eucharist, as spiritual food and drink.

Dear brothers and sisters, what happened in Mary also applies in ways that are different yet real to every man and to every woman because God asks each one of us to welcome him, to put at his disposal our heart and our body, our entire existence, our flesh, the Bible says, so that he may dwell in the world. He calls us to be united with him in the sacrament of the Eucharist, Bread broken for the life of the world, to form together the Church, his Body in history. And if we say 'yes', like Mary, indeed to the extent of our 'yes', this mysterious exchange is also brought about for us and in us. We are taken up into the divinity of the One who took on our humanity. The Eucharist is the means, the instrument of this reciprocal transformation which always has God as its goal, and as the main actor. He is the Head and we are the limbs, he is the Vine and we the branches. Whoever eats of this Bread and lives in communion with Jesus, letting himself be transformed by him and in him, is saved from eternal death: naturally he dies like everyone and also shares in the mystery of Christ's Passion and Crucifixion, but he is no longer a slave to death and will rise on the Last Day to enjoy the eternal celebration together with Mary and with all the Saints.

This mystery, this celebration of God, begins here below: it is the mystery of faith, hope and love that is celebrated in life and in the liturgy, especially that of the Eucharist, and is expressed in fraternal communion and in service for our neighbour. Let us pray the Blessed Virgin to help us always to nourish ourselves faithfully with the Bread of eternal life, so that, already on this earth, we may experience the joy of Heaven.

X
LOURDES

APOSTOLIC JOURNEY OF HIS HOLINESS BENEDICT XVI TO FRANCE ON THE OCCASION OF THE 150TH ANNIVERSARY OF THE APPARITIONS OF THE BLESSED VIRGIN MARY AT LOURDES, 12-15 SEPTEMBER 2008

From the Homily given for the

TORCHLIGHT PROCESSION

Lourdes, Rosary Square
Saturday, 13 September 2008

One hundred and fifty years ago, on 11 February 1858, in this place known as the Grotto of Massabielle, away from the town, a simple young girl from Lourdes, Bernadette Soubirous, saw a light, and in this light she saw a young lady who was "beautiful, more beautiful than any other". This woman addressed her with kindness and gentleness, with respect and trust: "She said *vous* to me", Bernadette recounted, "Would you do me the kindness of coming here for a fortnight?" she asked her. "She was looking at me as one person who speaks to another." It was in this conversation, in this dialogue marked by such delicacy, that the Lady instructed her to deliver certain very simple messages on prayer, penance and conversion. It is hardly surprising that Mary should be beautiful, given that – during the apparition of 25 March 1858 – she reveals her name in this way: "I am the Immaculate Conception."

Let us now look at this "woman clothed with the sun" (Rev

12:1) as she is described for us in Scripture. The Most Holy Virgin Mary, the glorious woman of the Apocalypse, wears on her head a crown of twelve stars which represent the twelve tribes of Israel, the entire people of God, the whole communion of Saints, while at her feet is the moon, image of death and mortality. Mary left death behind her; she is entirely re-clothed with life, the life of her Son, the risen Christ. She is thus the sign of the victory of love, of good and of God, giving our world the hope that it needs. This evening, let us turn our gaze towards Mary, so glorious and so human, allowing her to lead us towards God who is the victor.

Countless people have borne witness to this: when they encountered Bernadette's radiant face, it left a deep impression on their hearts and minds. Whether it was during the apparitions themselves or while she was recounting them, her face was simply shining. Bernadette from that time on had the light of Massabielle dwelling within her. The daily life of the Soubirous family was nevertheless a tale of deprivation and sadness, sickness and incomprehension, rejection and poverty. Even if there was no lack of love and warmth in family relationships, life at the *cachot* was hard. Nevertheless, the shadows of the earth did not prevent the light of heaven from shining. "The light shines in the darkness . . ." (Jn 1:5).

Lourdes is one of the places chosen by God for his beauty to be reflected with particular brightness, hence the importance here of the symbol of light. From the fourth apparition onwards, on arriving at the grotto, Bernadette would light a votive candle each morning and hold it in her left hand for as long as the Virgin was visible to her. Soon, people would give Bernadette a candle to plant in the ground inside the grotto. Very soon, too, people would place their own candles in this place of light and peace. The Mother of God herself let it be known that she liked the touching homage of these thousands of torches, which since that time have continued to shine upon the rock of the apparition and give her glory. From that day, before the grotto, night and day, summer and winter, a burning bush shines out, aflame with the prayers of pilgrims and the sick, who bring their concerns and their needs, but above all their faith and their hope.

By coming here to Lourdes on pilgrimage, we wish to enter, following in Bernadette's footsteps, into this extraordinary closeness between heaven and earth, which never fails and never ceases to grow. In the course of the apparitions, it is notable that Bernadette prays the rosary under the gaze of Mary, who unites herself to her at the moment of the doxology. This fact confirms the profoundly theocentric character of the prayer of the rosary. When we pray it, Mary offers us her heart and her gaze in order to contemplate the life of her Son, Jesus Christ. My venerable Predecessor, Pope John Paul II, came here to Lourdes on two occasions. In his life and ministry, we know how much his prayer relied upon the Virgin Mary's intercession. Like many of his predecessors in the Chair of Peter, he also keenly encouraged the prayer of the rosary; one of the particular ways in which he did so was by enriching the Holy Rosary with the meditation of the Mysteries of Light. These are now represented on the façade of the Basilica in the new mosaics inaugurated last year. As with all the events in the life of Christ, "which she preserved and pondered in her heart" (Lk 2:19), Mary helps us to understand all the stages in his public ministry as integral to the revelation of God's glory. May Lourdes, the land of light, continue to be a school for learning to pray the Rosary, which introduces the disciple of Jesus, under the gaze of his Mother, into an authentic and cordial dialogue with his Master!

On Bernadette's lips we hear the Virgin Mary asking us to *come here in procession* so as to pray with simplicity and fervour. The torchlight procession expresses the mystery of prayer in a form that our eyes of flesh can grasp: in the communion of the

Church, which unites the elect in heaven with pilgrims on earth, the light of dialogue between man and his Lord blazes forth and a luminous path opens up in human history, even in its darkest moments. This procession is a time of great ecclesial joy, but also a time of seriousness: the intentions we bring emphasize our profound communion with all those who suffer. We think of innocent victims who suffer from violence, war, terrorism, and famine; those who bear the consequences of injustices, scourges and disasters, hatred and oppression; of attacks on their human dignity and fundamental rights; on their freedom to act and think. We also think of those undergoing family problems or suffering caused by unemployment, illness, infirmity, loneliness, or their situation as immigrants. Nor must we forget those who suffer for the name of Christ and die for him.

Mary teaches us to pray, to make of our prayer an act of love for God and an act of fraternal charity. By praying with Mary, our heart welcomes those who suffer. How can our life not be transformed by this? Why should our whole life and being not become places of hospitality for our neighbours? Lourdes is a place of light because it is a place of communion, hope and conversion.

As night falls, Jesus says to us: "keep your lamps burning" (Lk 12:35); the lamp of faith, the lamp of prayer, the lamp of hope and love! This act of walking through the night, carrying the light, speaks powerfully to the depths of ourselves, touches our heart and says much more than any other word uttered or heard. This gesture itself summarizes our condition as Christians on a journey: we need light, and at the same time are called to be light. Sin makes us blind, it prevents us from putting ourselves forward as guides for our brothers and sisters, and it makes us unwilling to trust them to guide us. We need to be enlightened, and we repeat the prayer of blind Bartimaeus: "Master, let me receive my sight!" (Mk 10:51). Let me see my sin which holds me back, but above all, Lord, let me see your glory! We know that our prayer has already been granted and we give thanks because, as Saint Paul says in the Letter to the Ephesians, "Christ shall give you light" (5:14), and Saint Peter adds, "he called you out of darkness into his marvellous light" (1 Pet 2:9).

To us who are not the light, Christ can now say: "You are the light of the world" (Mt 5:14), entrusting us with the responsibility to cause the light of charity to shine. As the Apostle Saint John writes, "He who loves his brother abides in the light, and in him there is no cause for stumbling" (1 Jn 2:10). To live Christian love, means at the same time to introduce God's light into the world and to point out its true source. Saint Leo the Great writes: "Whoever, in fact, lives a holy and chaste life in the Church, whoever sets his mind on things that are above, not on things that are on earth (cf. Col 3:2), in a certain way resembles heavenly light; as long as he himself observes the brilliance of a holy life, he shows to many, like a star, the path that leads to God" (*Sermon* III:5).

In this shrine at Lourdes, to which the Christians of the whole world have turned their gaze since the Virgin Mary caused hope and love to shine here by giving pride of place to the sick, the poor and the little ones, we are invited to discover the simplicity of our vocation: it is enough to love.

Tomorrow, the celebration of the exaltation of the Holy Cross brings us into the very heart of this mystery. At this vigil, our gaze is already turned towards the sign of the new covenant on which the whole life of Jesus converges. The cross is the supreme and perfect act of the love of Jesus, who lays down his life for his friends. "So must the Son of man be lifted up, that whoever believes in him may have eternal life" (Jn 3:14-15).

As proclaimed in the songs of the Suffering Servant, the death of Jesus is a death which becomes a light for the nations; it is a death which, in intimate association with the liturgy of atonement, brings reconciliation, it is a death which marks the end of death. From that day onwards, the Cross is a sign of hope, Jesus' victory standard, "because God so loved the world that he gave his only Son, that whoever believes in him should not perish but have eternal life" (Jn 3:16). Through the Cross, our whole life gains light, strength and hope. The Cross reveals the whole depth of love contained in the original design of the Creator; through the Cross, all is healed and brought to completion. That is why life lived with faith in Christ dead and risen becomes light.

The apparitions were bathed in light and God chose to ignite in Bernadette's gaze a flame which converted countless hearts. How many come here to see it with the hope – secretly perhaps – of receiving some miracle; then, on the return journey, having had a spiritual experience of life in the Church, they change their outlook upon God, upon others and upon themselves. A small flame called hope, compassion, tenderness now dwells within them. A quiet encounter with Bernadette and the Virgin Mary can change a person's life, for they are here, in Massabielle, to lead us to Christ who is our life, our strength and our light. May the Virgin Mary and Saint Bernadette help you to live as children of light in order to testify, every day of your lives, that Christ is our light, our hope and our life!

APOSTOLIC JOURNEY OF HIS HOLINESS BENEDICT XVI TO FRANCE ON THE OCCASION OF THE 150TH ANNIVERSARY OF THE APPARITIONS OF THE BLESSED VIRGIN MARY AT LOURDES, 12-15 SEPTEMBER 2008

From the Homily given during the

EUCHARISTIC CELEBRATION

Prairie, Lourdes
Sunday, 14 September 2008

"Go and tell the priests that people should come here in procession, and that a chapel should be built here." This is the message Bernadette received from the "beautiful lady" in the apparition of 2 March 1858. For 150 years, pilgrims have never ceased to come to the grotto of Massabielle to hear the message of conversion and hope which is addressed to them. And we have done the same; here we are this morning at the feet of Mary, the Immaculate Virgin, eager to learn from her alongside little Bernadette. . .

"What a great thing it is to possess the Cross! He who possesses it possesses a treasure" (Saint Andrew of Crete, *Homily* X on the Exaltation of the Cross, PG 97, 1020). On this day when the Church's liturgy celebrates the feast of the Exaltation of the Holy Cross, the Gospel you have just heard reminds us of the meaning of this great mystery: God so loved the world that he gave his only Son, so that men might be saved (cf.

Jn 3:16). The Son of God became vulnerable, assuming the condition of a slave, obedient even to death, death on a cross (cf. Phil 2:8). By his Cross we are saved. The instrument of torture which, on Good Friday, manifested God's judgement on the world, has become a source of life, pardon, mercy, a sign of reconciliation and peace. "In order to be healed from sin, gaze upon Christ crucified!" said Saint Augustine (*Treatise on Saint John*, XII, 11). By raising our eyes towards the Crucified one, we adore him who came to take upon himself the sin of the world and to give us eternal life. And the Church invites us proudly to lift up this glorious Cross so that the world can see the full extent of the love of the Crucified one for mankind, for every man and woman. She invites us to give thanks to God because from a tree which brought death, life has burst out anew. On this wood Jesus reveals to us his sovereign majesty, he reveals to us that he is exalted in glory. Yes, "Come, let us adore him!" In our midst is he who loved us even to giving his life for us, he who invites every human being to draw near to him with trust.

This is the great mystery that Mary also entrusts to us this morning, inviting us to turn towards her Son. In fact, it is significant that, during the first apparition to Bernadette, Mary begins the encounter with the sign of the Cross. More than a simple sign, it is an initiation into the mysteries of the faith that Bernadette receives from Mary. The sign of the Cross is a kind of synthesis of our faith, for it tells how much God loves us; it tells us that there is a love in this world that is stronger than death, stronger than our weaknesses and sins. The power of love is stronger than the evil which threatens us. It is this mystery of the universality of God's love for men that Mary came to reveal here, in Lourdes. She invites all people of good will, all those who suffer in heart or body, to raise their eyes towards the Cross of Jesus, so as to discover there the source of life, the source of salvation.

The Church has received the mission of showing all people this loving face of God, manifested in Jesus Christ. Are we able to understand that in the Crucified One of Golgotha, our dignity as children of God, tarnished by sin, is restored to us? Let us turn our gaze towards Christ. It is he who will make us free to love as he loves us, and to build a reconciled world. For on this Cross, Jesus took upon himself the weight of all the sufferings and injustices of our humanity. He bore the humiliation and the discrimination, the torture suffered in many parts of the world by so many of our brothers and sisters for love of Christ. We entrust all this to Mary, mother of Jesus and our mother, present at the foot of the Cross.

In order to welcome into our lives this glorious Cross, the celebration of the Jubilee of Our Lady's apparitions in Lourdes urges us to embark upon a journey of faith and conversion. Today, Mary comes to meet us, so as to show us the way towards a renewal of life for our communities and for each one of us. By welcoming her Son, whom she presents to us, we are plunged into a living stream in which the faith can rediscover new vigour, in which the Church can be strengthened so as to proclaim the mystery of Christ ever more boldly. Jesus, born of Mary, is the Son of God, the sole Saviour of all people, living and acting in his Church and in the world. The Church is sent everywhere in the world to proclaim this unique message and to invite people to receive it through an authentic conversion of heart. This mission, entrusted by Jesus to his disciples, receives here, on the occasion of this Jubilee, a breath of new life. After the example of the great evangelizers from your country, may the missionary spirit which animated so many men and women from France over the centuries, continue to be your pride and your commitment!

When we follow the Jubilee Way* in the footsteps of Bernadette, we are reminded of the heart of the message of Lourdes. Bernadette is the eldest daughter of a very poor family, with neither knowledge nor power, and in poor health. Mary chose her to transmit her message of conversion, prayer and penance, in full accord with words of Jesus: "What you have hidden from the wise and understanding, you have revealed to babes" (Mt 11:25). On their spiritual journey, Christians too are called to render fruitful the grace of their Baptism, to nourish themselves with the Eucharist, to draw strength from prayer so as to bear witness and to express solidarity with all their fellow human beings (cf. *Homage to the Virgin Mary*, Piazza di Spagna, 8 December 2007). It is therefore a genuine catechesis that is being proposed to us in this way, under Mary's gaze. Let us allow her to instruct us too, and to guide us along the path that leads to the Kingdom of her Son.

In the course of her catechesis, the "beautiful lady" reveals her name to Bernadette: "I am the Immaculate Conception." Mary thereby discloses the extraordinary grace that she has received from God, that of having been conceived without sin, for "he has looked on his servant in her lowliness" (cf. Lk 1:48). Mary is the woman from this earth who gave herself totally to God, and who received the privilege of giving human life to his eternal Son. "Behold the handmaid of the Lord; let what you have said be done to me" (Lk 1:38). She is beauty transfigured, the image of the new humanity. By presenting herself in this way, in utter dependence upon God, Mary expresses in reality an attitude of total freedom, based upon the full recognition of her true

---

* The Jubilee Way is a walk that links four significant sites in the life of St Bernadette in Lourdes – the font where she was baptised, the *cachot* where she lived in 1858, the grotto of the apparitions, and the chapel of the hospice where she received her First Holy Communion.

dignity. This privilege concerns us too, for it discloses to us our own dignity as men and women, admittedly marked by sin, but saved in hope, a hope which allows us to face our daily life. This is the path which Mary opens up for man. To give oneself fully to God is to find the path of true freedom. For by turning towards God, man becomes himself. He rediscovers his original vocation as a person created in his image and likeness.

Dear Brothers and Sisters, the primary purpose of the shrine at Lourdes is to be a place of encounter with God in prayer and a place of service to our brothers and sisters, notably through the welcome given to the sick, the poor and all who suffer. In this place, Mary comes to us as a mother, always open to the needs of her children. Through the light which streams from her face, God's mercy is made manifest. Let us allow ourselves to be touched by her gaze, which tells us that we are all loved by God and never abandoned by him! Mary comes to remind us that prayer which is humble and intense, trusting and persevering, must have a central place in our Christian lives. Prayer is indispensable if we are to receive Christ's power. "People who pray are not wasting their time, even though the situation appears desperate and seems to call for action alone" (*Deus Caritas Est*, n.36). To allow oneself to become absorbed by activity runs the risk of depriving prayer of its specifically Christian character and its true efficacy. The prayer of the Rosary, so dear to Bernadette and to Lourdes pilgrims, concentrates within itself the depths of the Gospel message. It introduces us to contemplation of the face of Christ. From this prayer of the humble, we can draw an abundance of graces.

The presence of young people at Lourdes is also an important element. Dear friends, gathered this morning around the World Youth Day Cross: when Mary received the angel's visit, she was a young girl from Nazareth leading the simple and courageous life typical of the women of her village. And if God's gaze focussed particularly upon her, trusting in her, Mary wants to tell you once more that not one of you is unimportant in God's eyes. He directs his loving gaze upon each one of you and he calls you to a life that is happy and full of meaning. Do not allow yourselves to be discouraged by difficulties. Mary was disturbed by the message of the angel who came to tell her that she would become the Mother of the Saviour. She was conscious of her frailty in the face of God's omnipotence. Nevertheless, she said 'yes', without hesitating. And thanks to her yes, salvation came into the world, thereby changing the history of mankind. For your part, dear young people, do not be afraid to say yes to the Lord's summons when he invites you to walk in his footsteps. Respond generously to the Lord. Only he can fulfil the deepest aspirations of your heart. You have come to Lourdes in great numbers for attentive and generous service to the sick and to the other pilgrims, setting out in this way to follow Christ the servant. Serving our brothers and sisters opens our hearts and makes us available. In the silence of prayer, be prepared to confide in Mary, who spoke to Bernadette in a spirit of respect and trust towards her. May Mary help those who are called to marriage to discover the beauty of a genuine and profound love, lived as a reciprocal and faithful gift. To those among you whom he calls to follow him in the priesthood or the religious life, I would like to reiterate all the joy that is to be had through giving one's life totally for the service of God and others. May Christian families and communities be places where solid vocations can come to birth and grow, for the service of the Church and the world.

Mary's message is a message of hope for all men and women of our day, whatever their country of origin. I like to invoke Mary as the *star of hope* (*Spe Salvi*, n.50). On the paths of our lives, so often shrouded in darkness, she is a beacon of hope who enlightens us and gives direction to our journey. Through her 'yes', through the generous gift of herself, she has opened up to God the gates of our world and our history. And she invites us to live like her in invincible hope, refusing to believe those who claim that we are trapped in the fatal power of destiny. She accompanies us with her maternal presence amid the events of our personal lives, our family lives, and our national lives. Happy are those men and women who place their trust in him who, at the very moment when he was offering his life for our salvation, gave us his Mother to be our own.

May the Mother of the Lord always be honoured fervently in each of your families, in your religious communities and in your parishes! May Mary watch over all the inhabitants of your beautiful country and over the pilgrims who have come in such numbers from other countries to celebrate this Jubilee! May she be for all people the Mother who surrounds her children in their joys and their trials! Holy Mary, Mother of God, our Mother, teach us to believe, to hope and to love with you. Show us the way towards the kingdom of your Son Jesus. Star of the sea, shine upon us and lead us on our way! (cf. *Spe Salvi*, n.50). Amen.

APOSTOLIC JOURNEY OF HIS HOLINESS BENEDICT XVI TO FRANCE ON THE OCCASION OF THE 150TH ANNIVERSARY OF THE APPARITIONS OF THE BLESSED VIRGIN MARY AT LOURDES,
12-15 SEPTEMBER 2008

Homily given during the

EUCHARISTIC CELEBRATION FOR THE SICK

Esplanade in front of the Basilica of Notre-Dame du Rosaire, Lourdes
Monday, 15 September 2008

Yesterday we celebrated the Cross of Christ, the instrument of our salvation, which reveals the mercy of our God in all its fullness. The Cross is truly the place where God's compassion for our world is perfectly manifested. Today, as we celebrate the memorial of Our Lady of Sorrows, we contemplate Mary sharing her Son's compassion for sinners. As Saint Bernard declares, the Mother of Christ entered into the Passion of her Son through her compassion (cf. *Homily for Sunday in the Octave of the Assumption*). At the foot of the Cross, the prophecy of Simeon is fulfilled: her mother's heart is pierced through (cf. Lk 2:35) by the torment inflicted on the Innocent One born of her flesh. Just as Jesus cried (cf. Jn 11:35), so too Mary certainly cried over the tortured body of her Son. Her self-restraint, however, prevents us from plumbing the depths of her grief; the full extent of her suffering is merely suggested by the traditional symbol of the seven swords. As in the case of her Son Jesus, one might say that she too was led to perfection through this suffering (cf. Heb 2:10), so as to make her capable of receiving the new spiritual mission that her Son entrusts to her immediately before "giving up his spirit" (cf. Jn 19:30): that of becoming the mother of Christ in his members. In that hour, through the figure of the beloved disciple, Jesus presents each of his disciples to his Mother when he says to her: Behold your Son (cf. Jn 19:26-27).

Today Mary dwells in the joy and the glory of the Resurrection. The tears shed at the foot of the Cross have been transformed into a smile which nothing can wipe away, even as her maternal compassion towards us remains unchanged. The intervention of the Virgin Mary in offering succour throughout history testifies to this, and does not cease to call forth, in the people of God, an unshakable confidence in her: the *Memorare* prayer expresses this sentiment very well. Mary loves each of her children, giving particular attention to those who, like her Son at the hour of his Passion, are prey to suffering; she loves them quite simply because they are her children, according to the will of Christ on the Cross.

The psalmist, seeing from afar this maternal bond which unites the Mother of Christ with the people of faith, prophesies regarding the Virgin Mary that "the richest of the people . . . will seek your smile" (Ps 44:13). In this way, prompted by the inspired word of Scripture, Christians have always sought the smile of Our Lady, this smile which medieval artists were able to represent with such marvellous skill and to show to advantage. This smile of Mary is for all; but it is directed quite particularly to those who suffer, so that they can find comfort and solace therein. To seek Mary's smile is not an act of devotional or outmoded sentimentality, but rather the proper expression of the living and profoundly human relationship which binds us to her whom Christ gave us as our Mother.

To wish to contemplate this smile of the Virgin, does not mean letting oneself be led by an uncontrolled imagination. Scripture itself discloses it to us through the lips of Mary when she sings the Magnificat: "My soul glorifies the Lord, my spirit exults in God my Saviour" (Lk 1:46-47). When the Virgin Mary gives thanks to the Lord, she calls us to witness. Mary shares, as if by anticipation, with us, her future children, the joy that dwells in her heart, so that it can become ours. Every time we recite the Magnificat, we become witnesses of her smile. Here in Lourdes, in the course of the apparition of Wednesday 3 March 1858, Bernadette contemplated this smile of Mary in a most particular way. It was the first response that the Beautiful Lady gave to the young visionary who wanted to know who she was. Before introducing herself, some days later, as "the Immaculate Conception", Mary first taught Bernadette to know her smile, this being the most appropriate point of entry into the revelation of her mystery.

In the smile of the most eminent of all creatures, looking down on us, is reflected our dignity as children of God, that dignity which never abandons the sick person. This smile, a true reflection of God's tenderness, is the source of an invincible hope. Unfortunately we know only too well: the endurance of suffering can upset life's most stable equilibrium; it can shake the firmest foundations of confidence, and sometimes even leads people to despair of the meaning and value of life. There are struggles that we cannot sustain alone, without the help of divine grace. When speech can no longer find the right words, the need arises for a loving presence: we seek then the closeness not only of those who share the same blood or are linked to us by friendship, but also the closeness of those who are intimately bound to us by faith. Who could be more intimate to us than Christ and his holy Mother, the Immaculate One? More than any others, they are capable of understanding us and grasping how hard we have to fight against evil and suffering. The Letter to the Hebrews says of Christ that he "is not unable to sympathize with our weaknesses; for in every respect he has been tempted as we are" (cf. Heb 4:15). I would like to say, humbly, to those who suffer and to those who struggle and are tempted to turn their backs on life: turn towards Mary! Within the smile of the Virgin lies mysteriously hidden the strength to fight against sickness and for life. With her, equally, is found the grace to accept without fear or bitterness to leave this world at the hour chosen by God.

How true was the insight of that great French spiritual writer, Dom Jean-Baptiste Chautard, who, in *L'âme de tout apostolat*, proposed to the devout Christian to gaze frequently "into the eyes of the Virgin Mary". Yes, to seek the smile of the Virgin Mary is not a pious infantilism, it is the aspiration, as Psalm 44 says, of those who are "the richest of the people" (verse 13). "The richest", that is to say, in the order of faith, those who have attained the highest degree of spiritual maturity and know precisely how to acknowledge their weakness and their poverty before God. In the very simple manifestation of tenderness that we call a smile, we grasp that our sole wealth is the love God bears us, which passes through the heart of her who became our Mother. To seek this smile, is first of all to have grasped the gratuitousness of love; it is also to be able to elicit this smile through our efforts to live according to the word of her Beloved Son, just as a child seeks to elicit its mother's smile by doing what pleases her. And we know what pleases Mary, thanks to the words she spoke to the servants at Cana: "Do whatever he tells you" (cf. Jn 2:5).

Mary's smile is a spring of living water. "He who believes in me", says Jesus, "out of his heart shall flow rivers of living water" (Jn 7:38). Mary is the one who believed and, from her womb, rivers of living water have flowed forth to irrigate human history.

The spring that Mary pointed out to Bernadette here in Lourdes is the humble sign of this spiritual reality. From her believing heart, from her maternal heart, flows living water which purifies and heals. By immersing themselves in the baths at Lourdes, so many people have discovered and experienced the gentle maternal love of the Virgin Mary, becoming attached to her in order to bind themselves more closely to the Lord. In the liturgical sequence of this feast of Our Lady of Sorrows, Mary is honoured with the title of *Fons amoris*, "fount of love". From Mary's heart, there springs up a gratuitous love which calls forth a response of filial love, called to ever greater refinement. Like every mother, and better than every mother, Mary is the teacher of love. That is why so many sick people come here to Lourdes, to quench their thirst at the *"spring of love"* and to let themselves be led to the sole source of salvation, her son Jesus the Saviour.

Christ imparts his salvation by means of the sacraments, and especially in the case of those suffering from sickness or disability, by means of the grace of the Sacrament of the Sick. For each individual, suffering is always something alien. It can never be tamed. That is why it is hard to bear, and harder still – as certain great witnesses of Christ's holiness have done – to welcome it as a significant element in our vocation, or to accept, as Bernadette expressed it, to "suffer everything in silence in order to please Jesus." To be able to say that, it is necessary to have travelled a long way already in union with Jesus. Here and now, though, it is possible to entrust oneself to God's mercy, as manifested through the grace of the Sacrament of the Sick. Bernadette herself, in the course of a life that was often marked by sickness, received this sacrament four times. The grace of this sacrament consists in welcoming Christ the healer into ourselves. However, Christ is not a healer in the manner of the world. In order to heal us, he does not remain outside the suffering that is experienced; he eases it by coming to dwell within the one stricken by illness, to bear it and live it with him. Christ's presence comes to break the isolation which pain induces. Man no longer bears his burden alone: as a suffering member of Christ, he is conformed to Christ in his self-offering to the Father, and he participates, in him, in the coming to birth of the new creation.

Without the Lord's help, the yoke of sickness and suffering weighs down on us cruelly. By receiving the Sacrament of the Sick, we seek to carry no other yoke than that of Christ, strengthened through his promise to us that his yoke will be easy to carry and his burden light (cf. Mt 11:30). I invite those who are to receive the Sacrament of the Sick during this Mass to enter into a hope of this kind.

The Second Vatican Council presented Mary as the figure in whom the entire mystery of the Church is typified (cf. *Lumen Gentium*, nn.63-65). Her personal journey outlines the profile of the Church, which is called to be just as attentive to those who suffer as she herself was. I extend an affectionate greeting to those working in the areas of public health and nursing, as well as those who, in different ways, in hospitals and other institutions, are contributing to the care of the sick with competence and generosity. Equally, I should like to say to all the *hospitaliers*, the *brancardiers* and the carers who come from every diocese in France and from further afield, and who throughout the year attend the sick who come on pilgrimage to Lourdes, how much their service is appreciated. They are the arms of the servant Church. Finally, I wish to encourage those who, in the name of their faith, receive and visit the sick, especially in hospital chaplaincies, in parishes or, as here, at shrines. May you always sense in this important and delicate mission the effective and fraternal support of your communities. In this regard, I particularly greet and thank my brothers in the Episcopate, the French Bishops, Bishops and priests from afar, and all who serve the sick and suffering throughout the world. Thank you for your ministry close to our suffering Lord.

The service of charity that you offer is a Marian service. Mary entrusts her smile to you, so that you yourselves may become, in faithfulness to her son, springs of living water. Whatever you do, you do in the name of the Church, of which Mary is the purest image. May you carry her smile to everyone!

To conclude, I wish to join in the prayer of the pilgrims and the sick, and to pray with you a passage from the prayer to Mary that has been proposed for this Jubilee celebration:

"Because you are the smile of God, the reflection of the light of Christ, the dwelling place of the Holy Spirit,

Because you chose Bernadette in her lowliness, because you are the morning star, the gate of heaven and the first creature to experience the resurrection,

Our Lady of Lourdes", with our brothers and sisters whose hearts and bodies are in pain, we pray to you!

XI
AVE MARIA

Homily given at

FIRST VESPERS OF THE FIRST SUNDAY OF ADVENT

Saint Peter's Basilica
Saturday, 26 November 2005

With the celebration of First Vespers of the First Sunday in Advent we are beginning a new liturgical year. In singing the Psalms together, we have raised our hearts to God, placing ourselves in the spiritual attitude that marks this season of grace: "vigilance in prayer" and "exultation in praise" (cf. *Roman Missal*, Advent Preface, II/A).

Taking as our model Mary Most Holy, who teaches us to live by devoutly listening to the Word of God, let us reflect on the short Bible Reading just proclaimed.

It consists of two verses contained in the concluding part of the First Letter of St Paul to the Thessalonians (I Thes 5: 23-24). The first expresses the Apostle's greeting to the community: the second offers, as it were, the guarantee of its fulfilment.

The hope expressed is that each one may be made holy by God and preserved irreproachable in his entire person – "spirit, soul and body" – for the final coming of the Lord Jesus; the guarantee that this can happen is offered by the faithfulness of God himself, who will not fail to bring to completion the work he has begun in believers.

This First Letter to the Thessalonians is the first of all St Paul's Letters, written probably in the year 51. In this first Letter we can feel, more than in the others, the Apostle's pulsating heart, his paternal, indeed we can say maternal, love for this new community. And we also feel his anxious concern that the faith of this new church not die, surrounded as it was by a cultural context in many regards in opposition to the faith.

Thus, Paul ends his Letter with a hope, or we might almost say with a prayer. The content of the prayer we have heard is that they [the Thessalonians] should be holy and blameless at the coming of the Lord. The central word of this prayer is "coming". We should ask ourselves what does "coming of the Lord" mean? In Greek it is "parousia", in Latin "adventus", "advent", "coming". What is this "coming"? Does it involve us or not?

To understand the meaning of this word, hence, of the Apostle's prayer for this community and for communities of all times – also for us – we must look at the person through whom the coming of the Lord was uniquely brought about: the Virgin Mary.

Mary belonged to that part of the People of Israel who in Jesus' time were waiting with heartfelt expectation for the Saviour's coming. And from the words and acts recounted in the Gospel, we can see how she truly lived steeped in the Prophets' words; she entirely expected the Lord's coming.

She could not, however, have imagined how this coming would be brought about. Perhaps she expected a coming in glory. The moment when the Archangel Gabriel entered her house and told her that the Lord, the Saviour, wanted to take flesh in her, wanted to bring about his coming through her, must have been all the more surprising to her.

We can imagine the Virgin's apprehension. Mary, with a tremendous act of faith and obedience, said 'yes': "I am the servant of the Lord". And so it was that she became the "dwelling place" of the Lord, a true "temple" in the world and a "door" through which the Lord entered upon the earth.

We have said that this coming was unique: "the" coming of the Lord. Yet there is not only the final coming at the end of time: in a certain sense the Lord always wants to come through us. And he knocks at the door of our hearts: are you willing to give me your flesh, your time, your life?

This is the voice of the Lord who also wants to enter our epoch, he wants to enter human life through us. He also seeks a living dwelling place in our personal lives. This is the coming of the Lord. Let us once again learn this in the season of Advent: the Lord can also come among us.

Therefore we can say that this prayer, this hope, expressed by the Apostle, contains a fundamental truth that he seeks to inculcate in the faithful of the community he founded and that we can sum up as follows: God calls us to communion with him, which will be completely fulfilled in the return of Christ, and he himself strives to ensure that we will arrive prepared for this final and decisive encounter. The future is, so to speak, contained in the present, or better, in the presence of God himself, who in his unfailing love does not leave us on our own or abandon us even for an instant, just as a father and mother never stop caring for their children while they are growing up.

Before Christ who comes, men and women are defined in the whole of their being, which the Apostle sums up in the words "spirit, soul and body", thereby indicating the whole of the human person as a unit with somatic, psychic and spiritual dimensions. Sanctification is God's gift and his project, but human beings are called to respond with their entire being without excluding any part of themselves.

It is the Holy Spirit himself who formed in the Virgin's womb Jesus, the perfect Man, who brings God's marvellous plan to completion in the human person, first of all by transforming the heart and from this centre, all the rest.

Thus, the entire work of creation and redemption which God, Father and Son and Holy Spirit, continues to bring about, from the beginning to the end of the cosmos and of history, is summed up in every individual person. And since the first coming of Christ is at the centre of the history of humanity and at its end, his glorious return, so every personal existence is called to be measured against him – in a mysterious and multi-faceted way – during the earthly pilgrimage, in order to be found "in him" at the moment of his return.

May Mary Most Holy, the faithful Virgin, guide us to make this time of Advent and of the whole new liturgical year a path of genuine sanctification, to the praise and glory of God, Father, Son and Holy Spirit.

From the

MEETING OF THE HOLY FATHER BENEDICT XVI WITH THE CLERGY OF THE DIOCESES OF BELLUNO-FELTRE AND TREVISO

Church of St Justin Martyr, Auronzo di Cadore
Tuesday, 24 July 2007

All the Saints also always come with God. It is important – Sacred Scripture tell us from the very outset – that God never comes by himself but comes accompanied and surrounded by the Angels and Saints. In the great stained glass window in St Peter's which portrays the Holy Spirit, what I like so much is the fact that God is surrounded by a throng of Angels and living beings who are an expression, an emanation, so to speak, of God's love. And with God, with Christ, with the man who is God and with God who is man, Our Lady arrives. This is very important. God, the Lord, has a Mother and in his Mother we truly recognize God's motherly goodness. Our Lady, Mother of God, is the Help of Christians, she is our permanent comfort, our great help.

PASTORAL VISIT OF HIS HOLINESS BENEDICT XVI TO LORETO ON THE OCCASION OF THE *AGORÀ* OF ITALIAN YOUTH

From the Address given at the

PRAYER VIGIL WITH YOUNG PEOPLE

Plain of Montorso
Saturday, 1 September 2007

Let me tell you again this evening: if you stay united with Christ, each one of you will be able to do great things. This is why, dear friends, you must not be afraid to dream with your eyes open of important projects of good and you must not let yourselves be discouraged by difficulties. Christ has confidence in you and wants you to be able to realize all your most noble and lofty dreams of genuine happiness. Nothing is impossible for those who trust in God and entrust themselves to him.

Look at the young Mary; the Angel proposed something truly inconceivable to her: participation, in the most involving way possible, in the greatest of God's plans, the salvation of humanity. Facing this proposal, Mary, as we heard in the Gospel, was distressed for she realized the smallness of her being before the omnipotence of God; and she asked herself: "How is it possible? Why should it be me?" Yet, ready to do the divine will, she promptly said her 'yes' which changed her life and the history of all humanity. It is also thanks to her 'yes' that we are meeting here this evening.

I ask myself and I ask you: can God's requests to us, however demanding they may seem, ever compare with what God asked the young Mary? Dear young men and women, since Mary truly knows what it means to respond generously to the Lord's requests, let us learn from her to say our own 'yes'.

Mary, dear young people, knows your noblest and deepest aspirations. Above all, she well knows your great desire for love, with your need to love and to be loved. By looking at her, by following her docilely, you will discover the beauty of love; not a 'disposable' love that is transient and deceptive, imprisoned in a selfish and materialistic mindset, but true, deep love.

APOSTOLIC JOURNEY OF HIS HOLINESS BENEDICT XVI TO AUSTRIA ON THE OCCASION OF THE 850TH ANNIVERSARY OF THE FOUNDATION OF THE SHRINE OF MARIAZELL

From the Address given at the

PRAYER MEETING AT THE 'MARIENSÄULE'

Am Hof, Vienna, Friday, 7 September 2007

As the first stop of my pilgrimage to Mariazell I have chosen the *Mariensäule*, to reflect briefly with all of you on the significance of the Mother of God for Austria past and present, and her significance for each one of us. . . .

From earliest times, faith in Jesus Christ, the incarnate Son of God, has been linked to a particular veneration for his Mother, for the Woman in whose womb he took on our human nature, sharing even in the beating of her heart. Mary is the Woman who accompanied Jesus with sensitivity and deference throughout his life, even to his death on the Cross. At the end, he commended to her maternal love the beloved disciple and, with him, all humanity. In her maternal love, Mary continues to take under her protection people of all languages and cultures, and to lead them together, within a multiform unity, to Christ. In our problems and needs we can turn to Mary. Yet we must also learn from her to accept one another lovingly in the same way that she has accepted all of us: each as an individual, willed as such and loved by God. In God's universal family, in which there is a place for everyone, each person must develop his gifts for the good of all.

The *Mariensäule*, built by the Emperor Ferdinand III in thanksgiving for the liberation of Vienna from great danger and inaugurated by him exactly 360 years ago, must also be a sign of hope for us today. How many persons, over the years, have stood before this column and lifted their gaze to Mary in prayer! How many have experienced in times of trouble the power of her intercession! Our Christian hope includes much more than the mere fulfilment of our wishes and desires, great or small. We turn our gaze to Mary, because she points out to us the great hope to which we have been called (cf. Eph 1:18), because she personifies our true humanity.

This is what we have just heard in the Biblical Reading: even before the creation of the world, God chose us in Christ. From eternity he has known and loved each one of us. And why did he choose us? To be holy and immaculate before him in love. This is no impossible task: in Christ he has already brought it to fulfilment. We have been redeemed. By virtue of our communion with the Risen Christ, God has blessed us with every spiritual blessing. Let us open our hearts; let us accept this precious legacy. Then we will be able to sing, together with Mary, the praises of his glorious grace. And if we continue to bring our everyday concerns to the immaculate Mother of Christ, she will help us to open our little hopes ever more fully towards that great and true hope which gives meaning to our lives and is able to fill us with a deep and imperishable joy.

With these sentiments I would now like to join you in looking to Mary Immaculate, entrusting to her intercession the prayers which you have just now presented, and imploring her maternal protection upon this country and its people.

APOSTOLIC JOURNEY OF HIS HOLINESS BENEDICT XVI TO AUSTRIA ON THE OCCASION OF THE 850TH ANNIVERSARY OF THE FOUNDATION OF THE SHRINE OF MARIAZELL

Homily given at

HOLY MASS

Square in front of the Basilica of Mariazell
Saturday, 8 September 2007

With our great pilgrimage to Mariazell, we are celebrating the patronal feast of this Shrine, the feast of Our Lady's Birthday. For 850 years pilgrims have been travelling here from different peoples and nations; they come to pray for the intentions of their hearts and their homelands, bringing their deepest hopes and concerns. In this way Mariazell has become a place of peace and reconciled unity, not only for Austria, but far beyond her borders. Here we experience the consoling kindness of the Madonna. Here we meet Jesus Christ, in whom God is with us, as today's Gospel reminds us – Jesus, of whom we have just heard in the Reading from the prophet Micah: "He himself will be peace" (5:4). Today we join in the great centuries-old pilgrimage. We rest awhile with the Mother of the Lord, and we pray to her: Show us Jesus. Show to us pilgrims the one who is both the way and the destination: the truth and the life.

The Gospel passage we have just heard broadens our view. It presents the history of Israel from Abraham onwards as a pilgrimage, which, with its ups and downs, its paths and detours, leads us finally to Christ. The genealogy with its light and dark figures, its successes and failures, shows us that God can write straight even on the crooked lines of our history. God allows us our freedom, and yet in our failures he can always find new paths for his love. God does not fail. Hence this genealogy is a guarantee of God's faithfulness; a guarantee that God does not allow us to fall, and an invitation to direct our lives ever anew towards him, to walk ever anew towards Jesus Christ.

Making a pilgrimage means setting out in a particular direction, travelling towards a destination. This gives a beauty of its own even to the journey and to the effort involved. Among the pilgrims of Jesus's genealogy there were many who forgot the goal and wanted to make themselves the goal. Again and again, though, the Lord called forth people whose longing for the goal drove them forward, people who directed their whole lives towards it. The awakening of the Christian faith, the dawning of the Church of Jesus Christ was made possible, because there were people in Israel whose hearts were searching – people who did not rest content with custom, but who looked further ahead, in search of something greater: Zechariah, Elizabeth, Simeon, Anna, Mary and Joseph, the Twelve and many others. Because their hearts were expectant, they were able to recognize in Jesus the one whom God had sent, and thus they could become the beginning of his worldwide family. The Church of the Gentiles was made possible, because both in the Mediterranean area and in those parts of Asia to which the messengers of Jesus travelled, there were expectant people who were not satisfied by what everyone around them was doing and thinking, but who were seeking the star which could show them the way towards Truth itself, towards the living God.

We too need an open and restless heart like theirs. This is what pilgrimage is all about. Today as in the past, it is not enough to be more or less like everyone else and to think like everyone else. Our lives have a deeper purpose. We need God, the God who has shown us his face and opened his heart to us: Jesus Christ. Saint John rightly says of him that only he is God and rests close to the Father's heart (cf. Jn 1:18); thus only he, from deep within God himself, could reveal God to us – reveal to us who we are, from where we come and where we are going. Certainly, there are many great figures in history who have had beautiful and moving experiences of God. Yet these are still human experiences, and therefore finite. Only HE is God and therefore only HE is the bridge that truly brings God and man together. So if we Christians call him the one universal Mediator of salvation, valid for everyone and, ultimately, needed by everyone, this does not mean that we despise other religions, nor are we arrogantly absolutizing our own ideas; on the contrary, it means that we are gripped by him who has touched our hearts and lavished gifts upon us, so that we, in turn, can offer gifts to others. In fact, our faith is decisively opposed to the attitude of resignation that considers man incapable of truth – as if this were more than he could cope with. This attitude of resignation with regard to truth, I am convinced, lies at the heart of the crisis of the West, the crisis of Europe. If truth does not exist for man, then neither can he ultimately distinguish between good and evil. And then the great and wonderful discoveries of science become double-edged: they can open up significant possibilities for good, for the benefit of mankind, but also, as we see only too clearly, they can pose a terrible threat, involving the destruction of man and the world. We need truth. Yet admittedly, in the light of our history we are fearful that faith in the truth might entail intolerance. If we are gripped by this fear, which is historically well grounded, then it is time to look towards Jesus as we see him in the shrine at Mariazell. We see him here in two images: as the child in his Mother's arms, and above the high altar of the Basilica as the

Crucified. These two images in the Basilica tell us this: truth prevails not through external force, but it is humble and it yields itself to man only via the inner force of its veracity. Truth proves itself in love. It is never our property, never our product, just as love can never be produced, but only received and handed on as a gift. We need this inner force of truth. As Christians we trust this force of truth. We are its witnesses. We must hand it on as a gift in the same way as we have received it, as it has given itself to us.

'To gaze upon Christ' is the motto of this day. For one who is searching, this summons repeatedly turns into a spontaneous plea, a plea addressed especially to Mary, who has given us Christ as her Son: "Show us Jesus!" Let us make this prayer today with our whole heart; let us make this prayer above and beyond the present moment, as we inwardly seek the Face of the Redeemer. "Show us Jesus!" Mary responds, showing him to us in the first instance as a child. God has made himself small for us. God comes not with external force, but he comes in the powerlessness of his love, which is where his true strength lies. He places himself in our hands. He asks for our love. He invites us to become small ourselves, to come down from our high thrones and to learn to be childlike before God. He speaks to us informally. He asks us to trust him and thus to learn how to live in truth and love. The child Jesus naturally reminds us also of all the children in the world, in whom he wishes to come to us. Children who live in poverty; who are exploited as soldiers; who have never been able to experience the love of parents; sick and suffering children, but also those who are joyful and healthy. Europe has become child-poor: we want everything for ourselves, and place little trust in the future. Yet the earth will be deprived of a future only when the forces of the human heart and of reason illuminated by the heart are extinguished – when the face of God no longer shines upon the earth. Where God is, there is the future.

'To gaze upon Christ': let us look briefly now at the Crucified One above the high altar. God saved the world not by the sword, but by the Cross. In dying, Jesus extends his arms. This, in the first place, is the posture of the Passion, in which he lets himself be nailed to the Cross for us, in order to give us his life. Yet outstretched arms are also the posture of one who prays, the stance assumed by the priest when he extends his arms in prayer: Jesus transformed the Passion, his suffering and his death, into prayer, and in this way he transformed it into an act of love for God and for humanity. That, finally, is why the outstretched arms of the Crucified One are also a gesture of embracing, by which he draws us to himself, wishing to enfold us in his loving hands. In this way he is an image of the living God, he is God himself, and we may entrust ourselves to him.

'To gaze upon Christ!' If we do this, we realize that Christianity is more than and different from a moral code, from a series of requirements and laws. It is the gift of a friendship that lasts through life and death: "No longer do I call you servants, but friends" (Jn 15:15), the Lord says to his disciples. We entrust ourselves to this friendship. Yet precisely because Christianity is more than a moral system, because it is the gift of friendship, for this reason it also contains within itself great moral strength, which is so urgently needed today on account of the challenges of our time. If with Jesus Christ and his Church we constantly re-read the Ten Commandments of Sinai, entering into their full depth, then a great, valid and lasting teaching unfolds before us. The Ten Commandments are first and foremost a 'yes' to God, to a God who loves us and leads us, who carries us and yet allows us our freedom: indeed, it is he who makes our freedom real (the first three commandments). It is a 'yes' to the family (fourth commandment), a 'yes' to life (fifth commandment), a 'yes' to responsible love (sixth commandment), a 'yes' to solidarity, to social responsibility and to justice (seventh commandment), a 'yes' to truth (eighth commandment) and a 'yes' to respect for other people and for what is theirs (ninth and tenth commandments). By the strength of our friendship with the living God we live this manifold 'yes' and at the same time we carry it as a signpost into this world of ours today.

'Show us Jesus!' It was with this plea to the Mother of the Lord that we set off on our journey here. This same plea will accompany us as we return to our daily lives. And we know that Mary hears our prayer: yes, whenever we look towards Mary, she shows us Jesus. Thus we can find the right path, we can follow it step by step, filled with joyful confidence that the path leads into the light – into the joy of eternal Love. Amen.

From the Address given after the

RECITATION OF THE HOLY ROSARY

Basilica of Saint Mary Major
Saturday, 3 May 2008

In Rome this is the Marian temple par excellence, in which the people of the city venerate the icon of Mary *Salus Populi Romani* with great affection. I gladly welcomed the invitation addressed to me to lead the Holy Rosary on the First Saturday of the month of May, according to the beautiful tradition that I have had since my childhood. In fact, in my generation's experience, the evenings of May evoke sweet memories linked to the vespertine gatherings to honour the Blessed Mother. Indeed, how is it possible to forget praying the Rosary in the parish or in the courtyards of the houses and in the country lanes?

Today, together we confirm that the Holy Rosary is not a pious practice banished to the past, like prayers of other times thought of with nostalgia. Instead, the Rosary is experiencing a new Springtime. Without a doubt, this is one of the most eloquent signs of love that the young generation nourish for Jesus and his Mother, Mary. In the current world, so confused, this prayer helps to put Christ at the centre, as the Virgin did, who meditated within all that was said about her Son, and also what he did and said. When reciting the Rosary, the important and meaningful moments of salvation history are relived. The various steps of Christ's mission are traced. With Mary the heart is oriented toward the mystery of Jesus. Christ is put at the centre of our life, of our time, of our city, through the contemplation and meditation of his holy mysteries of joy, light, sorrow and glory. May Mary help us to welcome within ourselves the grace emanating from these mysteries, so that through us we can 'water' society, beginning with our daily relationships, and purifying them from so many negative forces, thus opening them to the newness of God. The Rosary, when it is prayed in an authentic way, not mechanical and superficial but profoundly, brings, in fact, peace and reconciliation. It contains within itself the healing power of the Most Holy Name of Jesus, invoked with faith and love at the centre of each 'Hail Mary'.

Dear brothers and sisters, let us thank God who has allowed us to live such a beautiful hour this evening, and in the following evenings of this Marian month, even if we will be far away, each in their own family and community, may we, just the same, feel close and united in prayer. Especially in these days that prepare us for the Solemnity of Pentecost, let us remain united with Mary, invoking for the Church a renewed effusion of the Holy Spirit. As at the origins, Mary Most Holy helps the faithful of every Christian community to form one heart and soul.

PASTORAL VISIT TO CAGLIARI – SARDINIA

From the Homily given during the

EUCHARISTIC CELEBRATION

Esplanade in front of the Shrine of Our Lady of Bonaria
Sunday, 7 September 2008

The most beautiful sight that a people can offer is without any doubt that of its own faith. At this moment I feel tangibly a moving manifestation of the faith that enlivens you and I would like immediately to express to you my admiration of this. I gladly accepted the invitation to come to your most beautiful island on the occasion of the centenary of the proclamation of Our Lady of Bonaria* as your principal Patroness. Today, together with the

* The Shrine of Our Lady of Bonaria is in Calgliari, Sardinia. According to tradition, on 25 March 1370 a ship travelling from Spain to Italy was caught in a terrible storm. The sailors, attempting to save the ship, began to cast its cargo into the sea. The last piece of cargo to have been dispatched was a large crate. The moment this crate hit the water the storm miraculously abated. The sailors attempted to retrieve this part of the cargo but to no avail. The crate eventually run aground on a beach at the foot of the hill of Bonaria. When the local people found it they discovered that they could neither move or open it until a child cried out, "Call for one of the Mercedarian Friars!" The Friars came and, without difficulty, lifted the crate and carried it into their church. When the friars opened the crate they discovered a beautiful statue of the Virgin and Child, the Virgin carrying a lighted candle in her right hand.

panorama of the wonderful nature that surrounds us, you offer me a view of your fervent devotion to the Most Holy Virgin. Thank you for this beautiful witness! . . .

It is the Lord's Day, but – given this special circumstance – the Liturgy of the Word has presented to us the Readings for the celebrations dedicated to the Blessed Virgin. These are, in particular, texts planned for the Feast of the Birth of Mary which for centuries has been fixed on 8 September, the date of the consecration of the basilica built in Jerusalem above the house of St Anne, Mother of Our Lady. They are Readings which effectively always contain the reference to the mystery of her birth. First of all there is the Prophet Micah's marvellous oracle concerning Bethlehem, in which the birth of the Messiah is announced. The Messiah, the oracle says, was to be a descendant of King David, like him a native of Bethlehem but a figure who would exceed human limitations: his "origin", it says, are "from ancient times", lost in the most remote ages, at the frontier of eternity. His greatness would reach "to the ends of the earth", as would also be his peace (cf. Mi 5: 1-4a). The coming of the "Lord's anointed", who was to mark the beginning of the people's liberation, was described by the Prophet with an enigmatic expression: "until the time when she who is in travail has brought forth" (Mi 5: 3). Thus the Liturgy – which is a privileged school of the faith – teaches us to see in Mary's birth a direct connection with that of the Messiah, Son of David.

The Gospel, a passage from the Apostle Matthew, presented to us precisely the account of Jesus' birth. However, the Evangelist introduces it with a summary of his genealogy, which he sets at the beginning as a prologue. Here too the full evidence of Mary's role in salvation history stands out: Mary's being is totally relative to Christ and in particular to his Incarnation. "Jacob the father of Joseph the husband of Mary, of whom Jesus was born, who is called Christ" (Mt 1: 16). The lack of continuity in the layout of the genealogy immediately meets the eye; we do not read 'begot' but instead: "Mary, of whom Jesus was born who is called Christ." Precisely in this we perceive the beauty of the plan of God who, respecting the human being, makes her fertile from within, causing the most beautiful fruit of his creative and redeeming work to develop in the humble Virgin of Nazareth. Then the Evangelist brings on stage the figure of Joseph, his inner drama, his robust faith and his exemplary rectitude. Behind Joseph's thoughts and deliberations is his love for God and his firm determination to obey him. But how is it possible not to feel that Joseph's distress, hence his prayers and his decision, were motivated at the same time by esteem and love for his betrothed? God's beauty and that of Mary are inseparable in Joseph's heart; he knows that there can be no contradiction between them; he seeks the answer in God and finds it in the light of the Word and of the Holy Spirit: "The Virgin shall be with child and give birth to a son, and they shall call him Emmanuel (which means, God with us)" (Mt 1: 23; cf. Is 7: 14).

Thus, once again, we can contemplate Mary's place in the saving plan of God, that 'purpose' which we find in the Second Reading, taken from the Letter to the Romans. Here the Apostle Paul expresses in two verses, unusually dense with meaning, the synthesis of what human life is from a meta-historical viewpoint: an arc of salvation that starts from God and returns to him; an arc entirely motivated and governed by his love. This is a salvific design totally permeated by divine freedom, which nonetheless awaits a fundamental contribution by human freedom: the creature's corresponds to the Creator's love. And it is here, in this space of human freedom, that we perceive the presence of the Virgin Mary, without her ever having been explicitly mentioned: she is in fact, in Christ, the first fruits and model of "those who love him [God]" (Rm 8: 28). The predestination of Mary is inscribed in the predestination of Jesus, as likewise is that of every human person. The "here I am" of the Mother faithfully echoes the "here I am" of the Son (cf. Heb 10: 6), as does the "here I am" of all adoptive children in the Son, that of us all, precisely.

Dear friends of Cagliari and Sardinia, thanks to their faith in Christ and through the spiritual motherhood of Mary and of the Church, your people too are called to be integrated in the spiritual 'genealogy' of the Gospel. . . . Indeed, we are here today to commemorate a great act of faith made by your ancestors a century ago when they entrusted their lives to the Mother of Christ, choosing her to be the most important Patroness of the island. They could not have known then that the twentieth century was to be a very difficult century but it was certainly in that consecration to Mary that they subsequently found the strength to face the difficulties that arose, especially with the two World Wars. It could only be like this. Your island, dear friends of Sardinia, could have no other protectress than Our Lady. She is the Mother, Daughter and Wife par excellence: *"Sa Mama, Fiza, Isposa de su Segnore"*, as you like to sing. She is the Mother who loves, protects, advises, consoles and gives life so that life may be born and endure. She is the Daughter who honours her family, is ever attentive to the needs of her brothers and sisters and is prompt in making her home beautiful and welcoming; she is the Wife capable of faithful, patient love, of sacrifice and of hope. In Sardinia at least 350 churches and shrines are dedicated to Mary. A people of mothers is reflected in that humble girl from Nazareth who with her 'yes' enabled the Word to become flesh.

I well know that Mary is in your hearts. A hundred years later, let us thank her today for her protection and renew our trust in her, recognizing her as the 'Star of the New Evangelization' at whose school we may learn how to bring Christ the Saviour to the men and women of our time.

May Mary help you to bring Christ to families, little domestic churches and cells of society, which today more than ever are in need of both spiritual and social trust and support. May she help you to find appropriate pastoral strategies to ensure that Christ is encountered by young people who by their nature bring new dynamism but often fall prey to the widespread nihilism, thirsting for truth and ideals precisely when they seem to deny them. May she render you capable of evangelizing the world of work, the economy and politics which need a new generation of committed lay Christians who can seek competently and with moral rigour sustainable solutions of development. In all these aspects of Christian commitment you can always count on the guidance and support of the Blessed Virgin. Let us therefore entrust ourselves to her maternal intercession.

Mary is the harbour, refuge and protection for the Sardinian people who have within them the strength of oak. When the storm has passed the oak stands strong; fires rage and it sends out new shoots; the drought comes and it wins through once again. Let us therefore renew joyfully our consecration to such a caring Mother. I am sure that generations of Sardinians will continue to climb to the Shrine at Bonaria to invoke the Virgin's protection. Those who entrust themselves to Our Lady of Bonaria, a merciful and powerful Mother, will never be disappointed. May Mary Queen of Peace and Star of Hope intercede for us. Amen!

From the

HOMILY GIVEN AT THE SQUARE OUTSIDE THE PONTIFICAL SHRINE OF POMPEII

Sunday, 19 October 2008

Following in the footsteps of the Servant of God John Paul II, today I have come on pilgrimage to Pompeii to venerate the Virgin Mary, Queen of the Holy Rosary, together with you.* I have come in particular to entrust to the Mother of God, in whose womb the Word was made flesh, the Assembly of the Synod of

---

* The Shrine of Our Lady of Pompeii was established by Blessed Bartolo Longo (1841-1926), a Satanist priest who repented and became a third order Dominican, taking the name Brother Rosario (Br Rosary). Having converted in 1871, Bartolo Longo was still concerned that he had not even begun to make amends for his past life but he remembered the words of a Dominican Father who had helped him to turn to Christ, that the Blessed Virgin Mary had told St Dominic that "he who propagates my Rosary will be saved." Thus Bartolo Longo began to assist in the preaching of the practice of the Rosary. In 1873 he restored a dilapidated church and initiated celebrations in honour of Our Lady of the Rosary. In 1875 he procured a very worn painting of Our Lady of the Rosary from a convent in Naples. He had the painting restored and soon miracles were reported to have been worked at the shrine. Bartolo Longo was beatified by Pope John Paul II on 26 October 1980, the Pope referring to him as the "Apostle of the Rosary". Pope John Paul II visited the shrine at Pompeii on 7 October 2003, the feast of Our Lady of the Rosary.

Bishops which is under way at the Vatican on the theme of 'The Word of God in the life and mission of the Church'. My Visit also coincides with World Mission Sunday; contemplating in Mary she who accepted within her the Word of God and gave him to the world, we shall pray at this Mass for all those in the Church who spend their energy in the service of proclaiming the Gospel to all the nations. . . .

Let us now allow [Mary], our mother and teacher, to guide us in reflecting on the Word of God that we have just heard. The First Reading and the Responsorial Psalm express the joy of the People of Israel at the salvation given by God, salvation that is liberation from evil and the hope of a new life. The oracle of Zephaniah is addressed to Israel who is designated with such names as "daughter of Zion" and "daughter of Jerusalem", and is invited to rejoice: "Sing aloud . . . rejoice and exult!" (Zep 3: 14). It is the same appeal that the Angel Gabriel addresses to Mary at Nazareth "Hail, full of grace" (Lk 1: 28). "Do not fear, O Zion" (Zep 3: 16), the Prophet says; "Do not be afraid, Mary" (Lk 1: 30), the Angel says. And the reason for trust is the same: "The Lord your God is in your midst; a warrior who gives victory" (Zep 3: 17), the Prophet says; "The Lord is with you" (Lk 1: 28), the Angel assures the Virgin. The Canticle of Isaiah also ends: "Shout and sing for joy, O inhabitant of Zion, for great in your midst is the Holy One of Israel" (Is 12: 6). The Lord's presence is a source of joy, for wherever he is, evil is overcome and life and peace triumph. I would like in particular to emphasize Zephaniah's wonderful expression, which in addressing Jerusalem says: the Lord "will renew you in his love" (3: 17). Yes, God's love has this power: to renew all things, starting from the human heart which is his masterpiece and in which the Holy Spirit best brings about his transforming action. With his grace, God renews man's heart, forgiving him his sins, reconciling him and instilling in him an impetus for good. All of this is expressed in the lives of the Saints and we see it here in particular in the apostolic work of Bl. Bartolo Longo, Founder of the new Pompeii. And so, in this hour, we open our hearts to this love, renewer of man and of all things.

From its beginnings, the Christian community has seen the personification of Israel and Jerusalem in a female figure as an important and prophetic approach to the Virgin Mary, who is recognized precisely as a "daughter of Zion" and the archetype of the people who "found grace" in the eyes of the Lord. This is an interpretation we find again in the Gospel account of the wedding feast at Cana (Jn 2: 1-11). The Evangelist John sheds symbolic light on the fact that Jesus is the Bridegroom of Israel, the new Israel that all of us are in faith, the spouse who has come to bring the grace of the new Covenant, represented by the "good wine". At the same time the Gospel emphasizes Mary's role, who at the beginning is called "the Mother of Jesus" but the Son himself later addresses her as "woman" and this has a very profound meaning: indeed, it implies that Jesus, to our wonder, before kinship places the spiritual bond according to which Mary herself personifies the beloved Bride of the Lord, that is, the People he has chosen to shower his blessings upon the whole human family. The symbol of the wine, together with that of the banquet, represents the theme of joy and of the feast. In addition, the wine, like the other biblical images of the vineyard and the vine, alludes metaphorically to love: God is the owner of the vineyard, Israel is the vineyard, a vineyard that will find its perfect fulfilment in Christ, of whom we are the branches; and the wine is the fruit, that is, love, because it is exactly love that God expects of his children. And we pray to the Lord, who has given Bartolo Longo the grace to bring love in this land, so that also our life and our heart bears this fruit of love and thus renews the earth. . . .

May this Shrine and this city continue above all to be ever

linked in a unique Marian gift: the prayer of the Rosary. When we see, in the famous painting of Our Lady of Pompeii, the Virgin Mother and the Child Jesus giving the Rosary beads to St Catherine of Siena and St Dominic respectively, we immediately understand that this prayer leads us through Mary to Jesus, as Pope John Paul II taught us in his Letter *Rosarium virginis Mariae,* in which he explicitly mentions Bl. Bartolo Longo and the charism of Pompeii. The Rosary is a spiritual 'weapon' in the battle against evil, against all violence, for peace in hearts, in families, in society and in the world.

Dear brothers and sisters, in this Eucharist, the inexhaustible source of life and hope, of personal and social renewal, let us thank God because in Bartolo Longo he has given us a luminous witness of this Gospel truth. And let us once again turn our hearts to Mary with the words of the Supplication that in a little while we shall be reciting together: "As our Mother, thou art our Advocate and our Hope. To thee, amidst sighs, do we lift up our hands, crying for mercy!" Amen.

From the Meditation given after the

RECITATION OF THE HOLY ROSARY

Pontifical Shrine of Pompeii
Sunday, 19 October 2008

Before entering the Shrine to recite the Holy Rosary with you, I paused briefly before the tomb of Bl. Bartolo Longo and, praying, I asked myself: "Where did this great apostle of Mary find the energy and perseverance he needed to bring such an impressive work, now known across the world, to completion? Was it not in the Rosary, which he accepted as a true gift from Our Lady's Heart?" Yes, that truly was how it happened! The experience of the Saints bears witness to it: this popular Marian prayer is a precious spiritual means to grow in intimacy with Jesus, and to learn at the school of the Blessed Virgin always to fulfil the divine will. It is contemplation of the mysteries of Christ in spiritual union with Mary, as the Servant of God Paul VI stressed in his Apostolic Exhortation *Marialis cultus* (n. 46), and as my venerable Predecessor John Paul II abundantly illustrated in his Apostolic Letter *Rosarium virginis Mariae*, that today I once again present in spirit to the community of Pompeii and to each one of you. You who live and work here in Pompeii, especially you, dear priests, men and women religious and lay people involved in this unique portion of the Church, are all called to make Bl. Bartolo Longo's charism your own and to become, to the extent and in the way that God grants to each one, authentic apostles of the Rosary.

To be apostles of the Rosary, however, it is necessary to

experience personally the beauty and depth of this prayer which is simple and accessible to everyone. It is first of all necessary to let the Blessed Virgin take one by the hand to contemplate the Face of Christ: a joyful, luminous, sorrowful and glorious Face. Those who, like Mary and with her, cherish and ponder the mysteries of Jesus assiduously, increasingly assimilate his sentiments and are conformed to him. In this regard, I would like to quote a beautiful thought of Bl. Bartolo Longo: "Just as two friends, frequently in each other's company, tend to develop similar habits", he wrote, "so too, by holding familiar converse with Jesus and the Blessed Virgin, by meditating on the mysteries of the Rosary and by living the same life in Holy Communion, we can become, to the extent of our lowliness, similar to them and can learn from these supreme models a life of humility, poverty, hiddenness, patience and perfection" (cited in *Rosarium virginis Mariae,* n. 15).

The Rosary is a school of contemplation and silence. At first glance, it could seem a prayer that accumulates words, therefore difficult to reconcile with the silence that is rightly recommended for meditation and contemplation. In fact, this cadent repetition of the *Hail Mary* does not disturb inner silence but indeed both demands and nourishes it. Similarly to what happens for the Psalms when one prays the Liturgy of the Hours, the silence surfaces through the words and sentences, not as emptiness, but rather as the presence of an ultimate meaning that transcends the words themselves and through them speaks to the heart. Thus, in reciting the *Hail Mary*, we must be careful that our voices do not 'cover' the voice of God who always speaks through the silence like the "still small voice" of a gentle breeze (1 Kgs 19: 12). Then how important it is to foster this silence full of God, both in one's personal recitation and in its recitation with the community. Even when the Rosary is prayed, as today, by great assemblies, and as you do in this Shrine every day, it must be perceived as a contemplative prayer. And this cannot happen without an atmosphere of inner silence.

I would like to add a further reflection concerning the Word of God in the Rosary, particularly appropriate in this period in which the Synod of Bishops is taking place on the theme: 'The Word of God in the life and mission of the Church'. If Christian contemplation cannot leave the Word of God out of consideration, if it is to be a contemplative prayer, the Rosary must always emerge from the silence of the heart as a response to the Word, after the model of Mary's prayer. Seen clearly, the Rosary is completely interwoven with scriptural elements. First of all there is the enunciation of the mystery, preferably made, as it has been today, with words taken from the Bible. The *Our Father* follows; by giving the prayer a "vertical" orientation, the soul of one who recites the Rosary is opened to the correct filial attitude in accordance with the Lord's invitation: "When you pray say: Father . . ." (Lk 11: 2). The first part of the *Hail Mary*, also taken from the Gospel, lets us listen again each time to the words that God addressed to the Virgin through the Angel and to the words of her cousin Elizabeth's blessing. The second part of the *Hail Mary* resounds like the answer of children who, in addressing supplications to their Mother, do nothing other than express their own adherence to the saving plan revealed by God. Thus the thought of those who pray remains ever anchored to Scripture and to the mysteries presented in it.

Lastly, remembering that today we are celebrating World Mission Sunday, I wish to recall the apostolic dimension of the Rosary, a dimension that Blessed Bartolo Longo lived intensely, drawing inspiration from it to carry out on this earth so many charitable initiatives and works of human and social promotion. Furthermore, he wanted this Shrine to be open to the whole world as a centre of outreach of the prayer of the Rosary and as a place of intercession for peace among peoples. Dear friends,

I would like to reinforce both of these aims: the apostolate of charity and prayer for peace, and I wish to confirm and entrust them once again to your spiritual and pastoral commitment. Following the example and with the support of the venerable Founder, never tire of working with enthusiasm in this part of the Lord's vineyard for which Our Lady has shown a special fondness.

PILGRIMAGE OF HIS HOLINESS
BENEDICT XVI TO THE HOLY LAND
8-15 MAY 2009

From the Homily given at

HOLY MASS

Mount Precipice – Nazareth
Thursday, 14 May 2009

"May the peace of the Risen Christ reign in your hearts, for as members of the one body you have been called to that peace!" (Col 3:15). With these words of the Apostle Paul, I greet all of you with affection in the Lord. I rejoice to have come to Nazareth, the place blessed by the mystery of the Annunciation, the place which witnessed the hidden years of Christ's growth in wisdom, age and grace (cf. Lk 2:52). . . .

Here in the home town of Jesus, Mary and Joseph, we have gathered to mark the conclusion of the Year of the Family celebrated by the Church in the Holy Land. As a sign of hope for the future I will bless the first stone of an International Centre for the Family to be built in Nazareth. Let us pray that the Centre will promote strong family life in this region, offer support and assistance to families everywhere, and encourage them in their irreplaceable mission to society.

This stage of my pilgrimage, I am confident, will draw the whole Church's attention to this town of Nazareth. All of us need, as Pope Paul VI said here, to return to Nazareth, to contemplate ever anew the silence and love of the Holy Family, the model of all Christian family life. Here, in the example of Mary, Joseph and Jesus, we come to appreciate even more fully the sacredness of the family, which in God's plan is based on the lifelong fidelity of a man and a woman consecrated by the marriage covenant and accepting of God's gift of new life. How much the men and women of our time need to reappropriate this fundamental truth, which stands at the foundation of society, and how important is the witness of married couples for the formation of sound consciences and the building of a civilization of love!

In today's first Reading, drawn from the book of Sirach (3:3-7, 14-17), the word of God presents the family as the first school of wisdom, a school which trains its members in the practice of those virtues which make for authentic happiness and lasting fulfilment. In God's plan for the family, the love of husband and wife bears fruit in new life, and finds daily expression in the loving efforts of parents to ensure an integral human and spiritual formation for their children. In the family each person, whether the smallest child or the oldest relative, is valued for himself or herself, and not seen simply as a means to some other end. Here we begin to glimpse something of the essential role of the family as the first building-block of a well-ordered and welcoming society. We also come to appreciate, within the wider community, the duty of the State to support families in their mission of education, to protect the institution of the family and its inherent rights, and to ensure that all families can live and flourish in conditions of dignity.

The Apostle Paul, writing to the Colossians, speaks instinctively of the family when he wishes to illustrate the virtues which build up the "one body" which is the Church. As "God's chosen ones, holy and beloved", we are called to live in harmony and peace with one another, showing above all forbearance and forgiveness, with love as the highest bond of perfection (cf. Col 3:12-14).

Just as in the marriage covenant, the love of man and woman is raised by grace to become a sharing in, and an expression of, the love of Christ and the Church (cf. Eph 5:32), so too the family, grounded in that love, is called to be a 'domestic church', a place of faith, of prayer and of loving concern for the true and enduring good of each of its members.

As we reflect on these realities here, in the town of the Annunciation, our thoughts naturally turn to Mary, "full of grace", the mother of the Holy Family and our Mother. Nazareth reminds us of our need to acknowledge and respect the God-given dignity and proper role of women, as well as their particular charisms and talents. Whether as mothers in families, as a vital presence in the work force and the institutions of society, or in the particular vocation of following our Lord by the evangelical counsels of chastity, poverty and obedience, women have an indispensable role in creating that "human ecology" (cf. *Centesimus Annus*, 39) which our world, and this land, so urgently needs: a milieu in which children learn to love and to cherish others, to be honest and respectful to all, to practise the virtues of mercy and forgiveness.

Here too, we think of Saint Joseph, the just man whom God wished to place over his household. From Joseph's strong and fatherly example Jesus learned the virtues of a manly piety, fidelity to one's word, integrity and hard work. In the carpenter of Nazareth he saw how authority placed at the service of love is infinitely more fruitful than the power which seeks to dominate. How much our world needs the example, guidance and quiet strength of men like Joseph!

Finally, in contemplating the Holy Family of Nazareth, we turn to the child Jesus, who in the home of Mary and Joseph grew in wisdom and understanding, until the day he began his public ministry. Here I would simply like to leave a particular thought with the young people here. The Second Vatican Council teaches that children have a special role to play in the growth of their parents in holiness (cf. *Gaudium et Spes*, n.48). I urge you to reflect on this, and to let the example of Jesus guide you, not only in showing respect for your parents, but also helping them to discover more fully the love which gives our lives their deepest meaning. In the Holy Family of Nazareth, it was Jesus who taught Mary and Joseph something of the greatness of the love of God his heavenly Father, the ultimate source of all love, the Father from whom every family in heaven and on earth takes its name (cf. Eph 3:14-15). . . .

"Let it be done to me according to your word" (Lk 1:38). May our Lady of the Annunciation, who courageously opened her heart to God's mysterious plan, and became the Mother of all believers, guide and sustain us by her prayers. May she obtain for us and our families the grace to open our ears to that word of the Lord which has the power to build us up (cf. Acts 20:32), to inspire courageous decisions, and to guide our feet into the path of peace!

PASTORAL VISIT TO BRESCIA AND CONCESIO

From the message given at the

ANGELUS

Paul VI Square – Brescia, Italy
Sunday, 8 November 2009

At this Angelus prayer, I wish to recall the profound devotion for the Virgin Mary of the Servant of God Giovanni Battista Montini. He celebrated his first Mass in the Shrine of Santa Maria delle Grazie, the Marian heart of your city, not far from this square. In this way he placed his priesthood under the maternal protection of the Mother of Jesus, and this bond accompanied him throughout his life.

As his ecclesial responsibilities grew, he developed an ever broader and more organic concept of the relationship between the Blessed Virgin Mary and the mystery of the Church. In this perspective, his closing *Discourse at the Third Session of the Second Vatican Council* on 21 November 1964 remains memorable. That session had promulgated the Constitution on the Church *Lumen Gentium*, which in the words of Paul VI "has as its summit and crown an entire chapter dedicated to Our Lady." The Pope noted that it was the most ample synthesis of Marian doctrine ever elaborated by an Ecumenical Council, aimed at "manifesting the face of the Holy Church, to which Mary is intimately bound" (*Enchiridion Vaticanum*, Bologna 1979, p. 185, nn. 300-302). In that context, he proclaimed Mary Most Holy as "Mother of the

Church" (cf. ibid., n. 306), emphasizing, with great ecumenical sensitivity, that "the devotion to Mary . . . is a means intended to orient souls towards Christ and thus to unite them with the Father, in the love of the Holy Spirit" (ibid., n. 315).

Echoing the words of Paul VI, today we too pray: O Virgin Mary, Mother of the Church, we entrust to you the Church of Brescia and the entire population of this region. Remember all your children; confirm their prayers to God; keep their faith steady; reinforce their hope; make charity grow. O merciful, O pious, O sweet Virgin Mary (cf. ibid., nn. 317, 320, 325).

XII
ORA PRO NOBIS

PRAYER OF HIS HOLINESS BENEDICT XVI BEFORE THE IMAGE OF OUR LADY OF GUADALUPE IN THE VATICAN GARDENS

11 May 2005

Holy Mary, who under the title of Our Lady of Guadalupe are invoked as Mother by the men and women of Mexico and of Latin America, encouraged by the love that you inspire in us, we once again place our life in your motherly hands.

May you, who are present in these Vatican Gardens, hold sway in the hearts of all the mothers of the world and in our own heart. With great hope, we turn to you and trust in you.

Hail Mary, full of grace,
the Lord is with thee,
blessed art thou among women
and blessed is the fruit of thy womb, Jesus.
Holy Mary, Mother of God,
pray for us sinners,
now and at the hour of our death. Amen.
Our Lady of Guadalupe, pray for us.

VISIT TO THE SHRINE OF LORETO AND PRIVATE PRAYER AT THE HOLY HOUSE

1 September 2007

Prayer

Mary, Mother of the 'Yes', you listened to Jesus,
and know the tone of his voice and the beating of his heart.
Morning Star, speak to us of him,
and tell us about your journey of following him on the path of faith.

Mary, who dwelt with Jesus in Nazareth,
impress on our lives your sentiments,
your docility, your attentive silence,
and make the Word flourish in genuinely free choices.

Mary, speak to us of Jesus, so that the freshness of our faith
shines in our eyes and warms the hearts of those we meet,
as you did when visiting Elizabeth,
who in her old age rejoiced with you for the gift of life.

Mary, Virgin of the *Magnificat*
help us to bring joy to the world and, as at Cana,
lead every young person involved in service of others
to do only what Jesus will tell them.

Mary, look upon the Assembly of youth,
so that the soil of the Italian Church will be fertile.
Pray that Jesus, dead and Risen, is reborn in us,
and transforms us into a night full of light, full of him.

Mary, Our Lady of Loreto, Gate of Heaven,
help us to lift our eyes on high.
We want to see Jesus, to speak with him,
to proclaim his love to all.

PRAYER TO OUR LADY OF SHESHAN

Day of Prayer for the Church in China, observed on 24 May 2008

Virgin Most Holy, Mother of the Incarnate Word and our Mother, venerated in the Shrine of Sheshan under the title 'Help of Christians', the entire Church in China looks to you with devout affection. We come before you today to implore your protection. Look upon the People of God and, with a mother's care, guide them along the paths of truth and love, so that they may always be a leaven of harmonious coexistence among all citizens.

When you obediently said 'yes' in the house of Nazareth, you allowed God's eternal Son to take flesh in your virginal womb and thus to begin in history the work of our redemption. You willingly and generously co-operated in that work, allowing the sword of pain to pierce your soul, until the supreme hour of the Cross, when you kept watch on Calvary, standing beside your Son, who died that we might live.

From that moment, you became, in a new way, the Mother of all those who receive your Son Jesus in faith and choose to follow in his footsteps by taking up his Cross. Mother of hope, in the darkness of Holy Saturday you journeyed with unfailing trust towards the dawn of Easter. Grant that your children may discern at all times, even those that are darkest, the signs of God's loving presence.

Our Lady of Sheshan, sustain all those in China, who, amid their daily trials, continue to believe, to hope, to love. May they never be afraid to speak of Jesus to the world, and of the world to Jesus. In the statue overlooking the Shrine you lift your Son on high, offering him to the world with open arms in a gesture of love. Help Catholics always to be credible witnesses to this love, ever clinging to the rock of Peter on which the Church is built. Mother of China and all Asia, pray for us, now and for ever. Amen!

VISIT TO THE CARITAS BABY HOSPITAL IN BETHLEHEM

Bethlehem, Wednesday, 13 May 2009

Mary, Health of the Sick, Refuge of Sinners, Mother of the Redeemer: we join the many generations who have called you "Blessed". Listen to your children as we call upon your name. You promised the three children of Fatima that "in the end, my Immaculate Heart will triumph". May it be so! May love triumph over hatred, solidarity over division, and peace over every form of violence! May the love you bore your Son teach us to love God with all our heart, strength and soul. May the Almighty show us his mercy, strengthen us with his power, and fill us with every good thing (cf. Lk 1:46-56). We ask your Son Jesus to bless these children and all children who suffer throughout the world. May they receive health of body, strength of mind, and peace of soul. But most of all, may they know that they are loved with a love which knows no bounds or limits: the love of Christ which surpasses all understanding (cf. Eph 3:19). Amen.

PRAYER TO OUR LADY OF THE OAK TREE IN VITERBO

6 September 2009

Holy Virgin, Our Lady of the Oak,
Patroness of the Diocese of Viterbo,
gathered together in this Shrine consecrated to you,
we extend to you a plea and a confident prayer:
Watch over the Successor of Peter
and over the Church entrusted to his care;
watch over this diocesan community and its pastors,
over Italy, over Europe and over the other continents.
Queen of Peace, obtain for us
the gift of harmony and peace
for all peoples and all mankind.

Obedient Virgin, Mother of Christ,
who, with your docile 'yes' to
the Angel's announcement,
became the Mother of the Almighty,
help all your children to follow
the plans that the heavenly Father
has for each one, in order
to cooperate in the universal plan
of redemption which Christ fulfilled
by dying on the Cross.

Virgin of Nazareth, Queen of the family,
make our Christian families schools of evangelical life,
enriched by the gift of many vocations
to the priesthood and to the consecrated life.

Keep intact the unity of our families,
today so threatened from all sides,
making them hearths of serenity and
of harmony, where patient dialogue
dispels difficulties and differences.
Above all, watch over those who are divided and in crisis,
Mother of forgiveness and reconciliation.

Immaculate Virgin, Mother of the Church,
nourish the enthusiasm of all members
of our Dioceses: of parishes and church groups,
of associations and new forms of apostolic commitment
that the Lord inspires with his Holy Spirit;
keep steadfast and determined
the will of those whom the Lord of the harvest
continues to call as labourers in his vineyard,
so that, resisting every worldly enticement and temptation,
they may persevere generously along the path they have taken,
and with your maternal aid, become witnesses to Christ
who are drawn by the splendour
of his Love, source of joy.

Clement Virgin, Mother of humanity,
turn your gaze to the men and women of our time,
to peoples and to those who govern them,
to nations and to continents;
comfort those who weep, who suffer,
who struggle because of human injustice;
sustain those who waver under the weight of effort
and who look at the future without hope;
encourage those who work to build a better world
where justice triumphs and brotherhood reigns,
where selfishness, hate and violence cease.
May every form and manifestation of violence

be conquered by the peace-making power of Christ.

Listening Virgin, Star of Hope,
Mother of Mercy,
the source through which
Jesus came into the world,
our life and our joy,
we thank you and we renew the offering of our lives,
certain that you will never abandon us,
especially in the dark and difficult moments of life.
Be with us always,
now and at the hour of our death.
Amen!

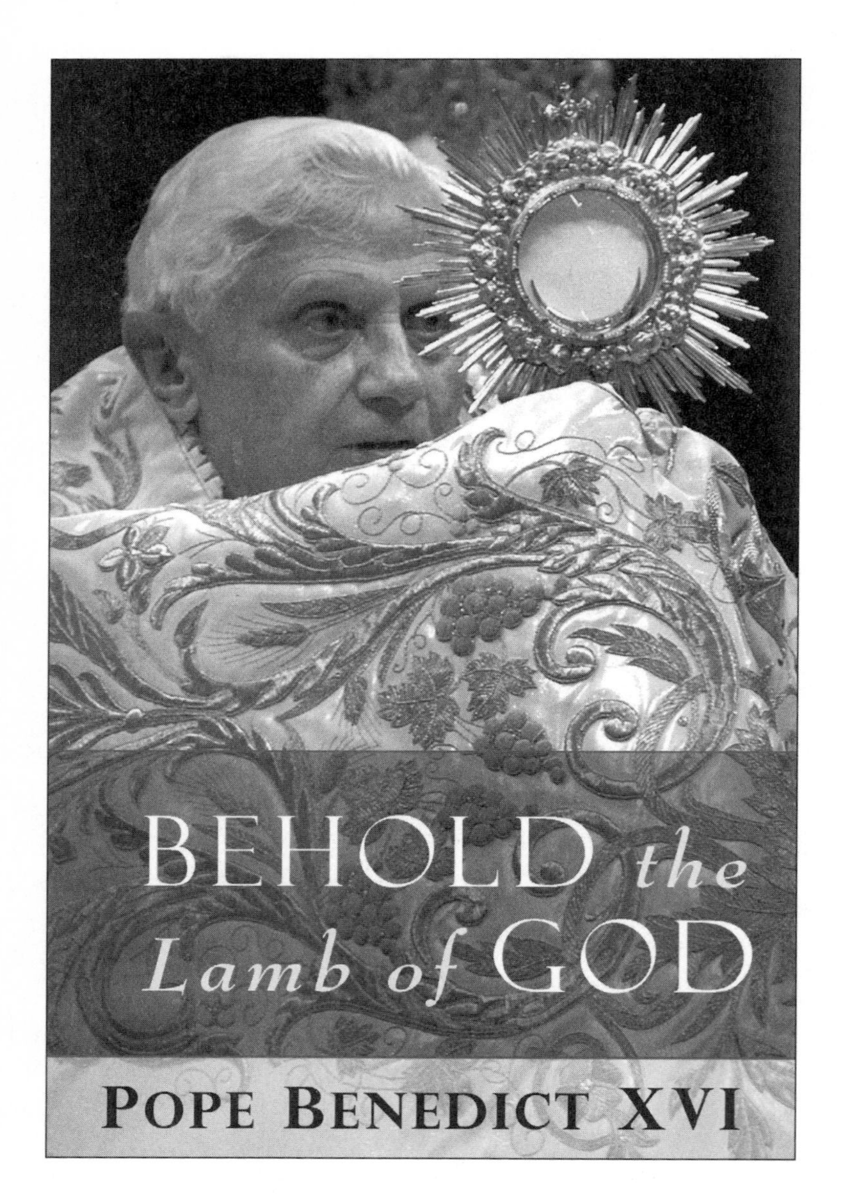
BEHOLD the
Lamb of GOD
POPE BENEDICT XVI

Reviews of *Behold the Lamb of God*

"Written with great pastoral sensitivity, this beautiful book is filled with deep spiritual and theological insight. . . . This latest book by the Holy Father will help both priests and laity gain a deeper understanding and appreciation of the Blessed Eucharist."

– Fr Miceal Beatty

"*Behold the Lamb of God* is a book that one could use for daily spiritual reading or as the text to inform a period of mental prayer or meditation. The Holy Father's homilies and addresses bear quiet and reflective reading, and can be a springboard for affective prayer and positive resolutions to live the Christian life more fully."

– Fr Tim Finigan

"The Pope's deep understanding and devotion is reflected in these extracts selected by Father Skinner from papal homilies delivered, in the main, on the feast days of Corpus Christi between 2005 and 2009, and from addresses and audiences given in Rome between 2006 and 2009. . . . The book costs a modest £8.95 – well worth the price if only for the single chapter, 'Homily given during Mass of the Lord's Supper, Holy Thursday, 9 April 2009'."

– Tim Matthews